7 SE

VISHNU

FROM THE HINDU TRINITY SERIES

Devdutt Pattanaik is a medical doctor by education, a leadership consultant by profession, and a mythologist by passion. He writes and lectures extensively on the relevance of stories, symbols and rituals in modern life. He has written over fifteen books, which include *7 Secrets of Hindu Calendar Art* (Westland), *Myth=Mithya: A Handbook of Hindu Mythology* (Penguin), *Book of Ram* (Penguin), *Jaya: An Illustrated Retelling of the Mahabharata* (Penguin).

To know more visit devdutt.com

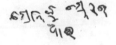

7 SECRETS

OF

VISHNU

FROM THE HINDU TRINITY SERIES

DEVDUTT PATTANAIK

𝓌

westland publications ltd

61, II Floor, Silverline Building, Alapakkam Main Road, Maduravoyal, Chennai 600095

93, I Floor, Sham Lal Road, Daryaganj, New Delhi 110002

First published by westland ltd 2011

This edition published by westland ltd 2016

This edition first published by westland publications ltd 2017

Copyright © Devdutt Pattanaik 2011

10 9 8 7 6 5 4 3

ISBN: 978-93-86224-05-7

Typeset and designed by Special Effects, Mumbai

Printed at Thomson Press (India) Ltd.

I humbly and most respectfully dedicate this book to those hundreds of artists and artisans who made sacred art so easily accessible to the common man

CONTENTS

Author's Note: On communicating
ideas   ix

1. Mohini's Secret   1

2. Matsya's Secret   37

3. Kurma's Secret   59

4. Trivikrama's Secret   91

5. Ram's Secret   127

6. Krishna's Secret   157

7. Kalki's Secret   195

Acknowledgements   219

CONTENTS

AUTHOR'S NOTE
On communicating ideas

It is significant that the stories of Vishnu rose to prominence after the rise of Buddhism. Prior to that, Hinduism was a religion of elite-based complex rituals known as yagna, and esoteric speculations captured in texts known as the Aranyakas and the Upanishads. These seemed very distant to the common man who focused on fertility rituals, worship of plants and animals and nature.

Buddhism spoke directly to the common man in the language of the people and addressed everyday concerns. It naturally became very popular. But the Buddhist worldview leaned towards monasticism. By contrast, the Hindu worldview made room for both the hermit and the householder. To fire the imagination of people moving towards monasticism, this had to be communicated using a tool that the masses relished — stories.

Stories of Vishnu communicate the Hindu worldview from the point of view of the householder. This is complemented by stories of Shiva that communicate an equally valid but alternate viewpoint, that of the hermit. Since both Vishnu and Shiva were forms of God, both worldviews, that of the householder and that of the hermit, were held in equal regard.

To ensure that these stories were not reduced to entertainment, they were deemed sacred and anchored with symbols and rituals. The symbols and rituals of Vishnu are different from the symbols and rituals of Shiva. For example,

Vishnu is visualised bedecked in gold while Shiva is worshipped smeared in ash; Vishnu is offered sprigs of the tulsi that is grown inside the house while Shiva is offered leaves of the bilva that is grown outside the house; Vishnu dances with his eyes open while Shiva dances with his eyes shut. Through these differences, different ideas were communicated.

Wisdom that was once restricted to a few now reached everyone who chose to hear the stories, look at the symbols, and perform the rituals. Vishnu represents a key figure in the new story-based Hinduism. He is a critical piece of what can be called the grand Hindu jigsaw puzzle.

To help readers unravel the secrets of Vishnu, the chapters have been arranged as below:

- The first chapter focuses on how gender is used to explain fundamental metaphysical concepts integral to Hinduism.

- The second chapter discusses the difference between man and animal.

- The third and fourth chapters focus on the Devas and the Asuras, both of whom are unhappy, as one struggles with insecurity and the other with ambition.

- The fifth and sixth chapters revolve around the *Ramayana* and *Mahabharata*, as man struggles with his humanity.

- The seventh chapter is about the wisdom of letting go with faith in renewal.

- This book seeks to make explicit patterns that are implicit in stories, symbols and rituals of Vishnu firm in the belief that:

Within Infinite Truths lies the Eternal Truth
Who sees it all?
Varuna has but a thousand eyes
Indra, a hundred
And I, only two

1
MOHINI'S SECRET
Spiritual growth need not
exclude material growth

The clothes and hairstyle are of a woman though the image is identified as Vishnu, the male householder form of God.

A festival image or utsav-moorti of Vishnu as Mohini from a south Indian temple

Mohini is the female form of Vishnu. She is an enchantress, an alluring damsel, a temptress. But she is not a nymph, or Apsara, such as Menaka, Rambha and Urvashi, renowned in Hindu mythology for their ability to seduce sages and demons. Mohini stands apart because she is identified as Vishnu and Vishnu is conventionally visualised as male. Mohini is his female form.

Hindu mythology uses gender as a vehicle to communicate metaphysical ideas. A fundamental theme in Indian metaphysics is the existence of two realities: material reality and spiritual reality. Material reality is tangible reality that can be perceived through the senses. Spiritual reality is intangible reality that cannot be perceived through the senses. Material reality is represented using female form while spiritual reality is represented using male form.

Mohini is female in form but male in essence, unlike Apsaras who are totally female. Both enchant, but their intentions are different. An Apsara enchants to distract humanity from spiritual reality and entrap all in material reality. Mohini enchants to draw humanity's attention to spiritual reality within material reality. Mohini is thus spiritual reality wrapped in material reality. This is the central theme of Vishnu lore.

IN METAPHYSICS, MATERIAL REALITY IS known as prakriti, and spiritual reality is referred to as purusha. Prakriti means nature. Purusha means human.

Humans are accorded a special place in nature over minerals, plants and animals, because only humans have the ability to reflect, introspect, imagine and choose. All these qualities

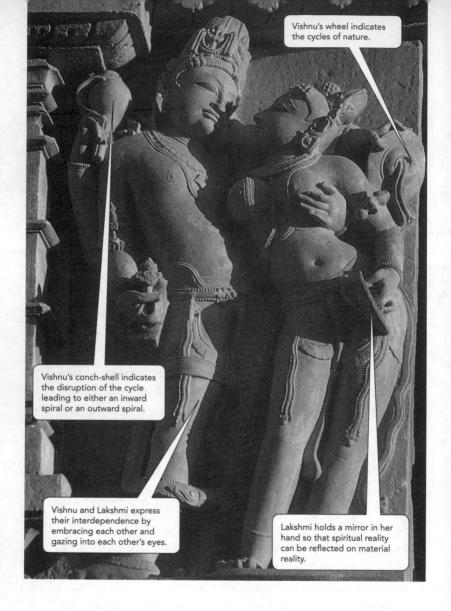

Vishnu's wheel indicates the cycles of nature.

Vishnu's conch-shell indicates the disruption of the cycle leading to either an inward spiral or an outward spiral.

Vishnu and Lakshmi express their interdependence by embracing each other and gazing into each other's eyes.

Lakshmi holds a mirror in her hand so that spiritual reality can be reflected on material reality.

Vishnu and Lakshmi on the walls of a Khajuraho temple, built in the 12th century, by Chandela kings

make it possible for humans to rise above physical limitations, transcend the boundaries of nature, and discover infinity. Human life is thus special. Therefore, the ancients represented both metaphysical principles using human symbols.

Material and spiritual reality are interdependent. Without material reality, spiritual reality cannot be discovered, and without spiritual reality, material reality has no purpose. This idea of complementary realities is expressed in Hindu mythology as a human couple. The interdependence of material and spiritual reality is best expressed through the interdependence of woman and man. This is the reason why temple walls are adorned with intimate conjugal images or dampatya.

In the Puranas, common nouns become proper nouns; an idea becomes a god or a goddess. Thus purusha becomes Purusha, or God, and prakriti becomes Prakriti, or Mother Nature. In Vishnu lore, Purusha is called Vishnu while Prakriti is called Lakshmi. He sustains the world; she is wealth personified. He cannot perform his role without her and she has no role without him. He gives her purpose and she gives him wherewithal. Thus Vishnu and Lakshmi validate each other. One cannot exist without the other.

BUT THE MYTHOLOGICAL ASSOCIATION OF women with material reality irks many people. Why not the other way round? Why not represent spiritual reality through Lakshmi and material reality through Vishnu?

The reason for the irritation lies in the tendency to place spiritual reality on a higher plane than material reality. When this is coupled with the subordinate position of women in a

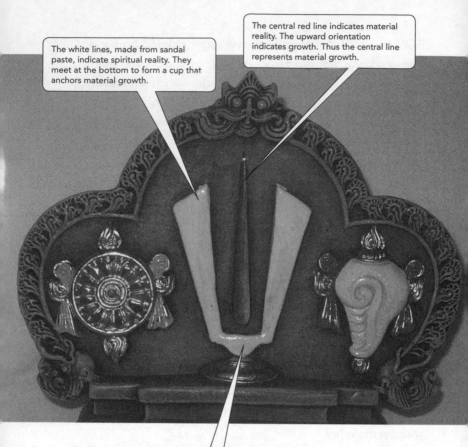

The white lines, made from sandal paste, indicate spiritual reality. They meet at the bottom to form a cup that anchors material growth.

The central red line indicates material reality. The upward orientation indicates growth. Thus the central line represents material growth.

Making sandal paste demands tremendous faith and patience. It takes years before the wood of the tree can produce fragrant paste. The wood of a mature tree has to be rubbed on a wet surface in rhythmic circular motion. The more one rubs, the more paste one gets. At first the paste is transparent and the sandal invisible, but one must have faith. In time, the water evaporates and the sandal colour will be seen.

The sacred mark of Vishnu or the urdhva-namam or the vertical mark

male-dominated society, it seems that the use of women to represent material reality is yet another attempt to impose patriarchal values. However, this is not true. Yes, mythological scriptures do use the female form to depict material reality, but the reason has less to do with gender politics and more to do with human physiology.

The fundamental difference between a man's body and a woman's body is that a man creates life outside his body while a woman creates life inside her body. He provides the trigger to life; she gives form to life. Both are essential to life in different ways. In metaphysics, spiritual reality triggers the observation while material reality embodies observation. The male body is doing in the reproductive context what spiritual reality is doing at a metaphysical context. So is the case with the female body. The male body is therefore best suited to represent spiritual reality while the female body is best suited to represent material reality. This does not mean men are spiritual and women are materialistic. In mythology, all forms are symbolic.

VISHNU'S SACRED MARK, THE VERTICAL namam, includes both material as well as spiritual reality. Material reality is represented by red, the colour of blood that sustains life as it flows through the veins. Spiritual reality is represented by white, the colour of bones that upholds life by being still.

The central red line and the adjacent white lines are oriented upwards indicating growth. From the verb 'to grow', which is 'Brh' in Sanskrit, comes the Vedic word for God, which is brahman. Brahman is that which grows, that which is vast, that which is infinite. Vishnu means 'that which expands to occupy

Venkateshwara Balaji of Tirupati, Andhra Pradesh

everything'. In other words, Vishnu is God who celebrates infinite growth, both material and spiritual.

What does material growth mean? It means access to all the wonderful things the material world has to offer to please the five senses: food, clothing, shelter, music, dance, art, entertainment, relationships, peace, pleasure and prosperity. A visit to any Vishnu temple — whether it is Venkateshwara Balaji in Tirupati, or Srinathji in Rajasthan or Jagannath in Puri or the grand complexes of Ranganatha on the river-islands of the Kaveri — shows how material splendour is an intrinsic part of Vishnu worship. The rituals include colour and fragrance and music and flavours.

But material things are impermanent. Sooner or later, they wither away or cease to pleasure the mind. This causes pain, frustration, anxiety, stress, insecurity and fear, emotions that are most undesirable. Left unchecked, they can evoke in the mind greed and jealousy, rage and attachment.

Spiritual growth is the ability to overpower these emotions so that one has the wisdom to appreciate and enjoy all things material without getting needy or clingy. One is happy when the material world favours us and not unhappy when it does not. This can only happen when material growth is accompanied by intellectual growth. Only intellectual growth can control emotional turmoil caused by dependence on material things.

This is why the sacred mark of Vishnu is placed on the head, container of the human intellect. That is why the two white lines of spirituality form a cup at the base to anchor and support the single red line of materialism that stretches upwards in aspiration. Fetterless material growth is not a desired state.

An image from Nepal known as Budhanilakantha that is
Vishnu as Narayana sleeping on the serpent Sesha

Temple wall sculpture from Belur, Karnataka, showing
Vishnu seated on the serpent Ananta

THE FIRST STEP IN THE pursuit of spiritual reality is to take birth as a human being, for only the flesh can sense material reality and only human flesh can fathom spiritual reality.

Perhaps it is the idea of an unborn human child floating in the water of its mother's womb that inspires the visualisation of Narayana, a form of Vishnu that sleeps on the waters. When Vishnu slumbers, the world does not exist, in form, or in thought. So it is with the unborn child.

In the unborn state, the child is innocent and ignorant of the world outside. It is not exposed to the form of the world, nor does it have any thoughts on the world. No thoughts on spirit or matter, no thoughts of male or female, white or red. Nothing. The unborn child is like Narayana in dreamless slumber.

Narayana sleeps on the coils of a serpent with many hoods. This serpent is called Adi-Ananta-Sesha, and it represents time. Adi means primal, Ananta means infinite and Sesha means the residue. These three names refer to three states of time corresponding to when one is awakening, when one is awake and when one is slumbering. When we awake, we first sense the flow of time. This is Adi, the primal sensation, represented mathematically as one, the first number. When we are fully awake, we can potentially perceive the world in infinite ways. This is Ananta, the ultimate sensation, represented mathematically as infinity. While we are in deep slumber and do not dream, we have no sense of time, hence no perception of the world. Nothing exists. What remains then is nothingness or Sesha, the residue, equal to what is mathematically represented by the number zero. Thus the name of Vishnu's serpent, Adi-Ananta-Sesha, draws attention to the three states of being all human beings go through cyclically: awakening, waking and slumber states.

Calendar art showing Brahma rising from Vishnu's navel

WHEN NARAYANA AWAKENS, A LOTUS blooms from his navel. In it sits Brahma.

Brahma is the child slipping out of the mother's womb. He senses the sudden rush of stimuli from the outside world. It is different from the experience in his mother's womb. This is his first brush with nature.

Brahma recognises himself as distinct from Prakriti. This ability comes from Purusha within him, but he does not know it yet. He knows he is not Prakriti. He objectifies nature as he becomes increasingly self-aware. The birth of Brahma thus marks the birth of human consciousness.

Brahma represents consciousness that is finite; it has the capability to realise infinite consciousness which is brahman. Hence the Vedic maxim, 'Aham Brahmasmi', which means both 'I am Brahma' as well as 'I am brahman'. The first meaning is acknowledgment of the finite truth that has been unravelled. The second meaning is the aspiration for the infinite truth that awaits unravelling.

The human mind, or Brahma, observes that nature is never still. As one moves from place to place, nature changes: wet rainy forests turn into deserts, cold icy mountains turn into vast oceans. Even when one sits in a place, one observes nature restless, changing with time: plants wither and die, animals mate and migrate, seasons change, sun rises and sets, moon waxes and wanes, the celestial sphere rotates around the Pole Star. Everything that is born eventually dies.

In the mother's womb everything is static and comfortable. Nothing is expected. But outside, in nature, everything is moving, and one is expected to act if one has to survive. As far as Brahma is concerned, Prakriti is Shatarupa, the restless goddess

Narayana embodies infinite reality. The deity is param-atma.

Through each doorway one can see only a portion of the deity, indicating that humans have access only to a limited vision of infinite reality. The devotee is jiva-atma.

Calendar art depicting the inner shrine of the temple at Thiruvananthapuram, where lies a giant image of Padmanabhaswami

with myriad forms. She frightens him.

BRAHMA'S MIND IS BLESSED WITH manas or imagination. He is able to imagine a time Shatarupa dances to his whims. This gives him joy. He is also able to imagine a time when Shatarupa overwhelms him. This frightens him. Most critically, he is able to imagine a time when he will not be able to experience Shatarupa. In other words, he imagines death. This frightens him the most.

Brahma passes on this fear of mortality to all living creatures, the jiva-atma, who are his children and his grandchildren. That is why all babies cry when they are born. That is why Brahma is not worshipped.

Vishnu has no such fear. He knows that what Brahma considers death is merely the death of the body that encases the Purusha. He does not depend on material reality for his identity. He knows that he is Purusha, infinite and immortal. He is param-atma. That is why Vishnu is worshipped. He is what all jiva-atma aspire to be.

Brahma shuns those aspects of nature that frighten him and he yearns for those aspects of nature that comfort him. This shunning of fear and yearning for comfort gives birth to a goddess called Maya.

The word Maya has its root in 'Ma' which means 'to measure'. Maya is a measuring scale. Like Prakriti, Maya is an aspect of material reality. But while Prakriti is physical, Maya is mental. Prakriti existed before Brahma, Maya comes after. Prakriti is Brahma's mother while Maya is his daughter; or one can say wife, because Brahma does not know he created Maya.

Brahma needs Maya to survive Prakriti. Brahma observes

Mysore painting showing the goddess Maya watching over the reclining Vishnu

Prakriti, and tries to make sense of her, through the lens of Maya. Maya is the measuring scale. Brahma is doing the measuring. Prakriti is that which he measures. With the help of Maya, Brahma is able to judge Prakriti as good or bad, right or wrong, beautiful or ugly. No more is Brahma intimidated by Shatarupa and her transformations. This ability to judge the world around him makes Brahma feel very powerful.

UNFORTUNATELY MAYA IS NOT STATIC. She is continuously informed and coloured by Brahma's experiences and expectations. When experience changes, when expectation changes, Maya recalibrates herself. As a result, what was right in the past may be wrong in the future; what was good in one part of the world may be bad in the other; what one person may find beautiful may be ugly for another. This confuses and confounds Brahma. It leads to conflicts between his children. One wonders what the perfect truth is. One questions reality. One wonders what the point of life is. This amplifies fear.

Maya often is taken to mean delusion. A world seen through a measuring scale is a delusion, because it is a perception, dependent on a measuring scale. It is a delusion that comforts Brahma as well as perplexes him. Without it, Brahma is lost. With it, he has meaning, purpose and direction.

The world of delusion constructed by Brahma with the help of Maya is called Brahmanda or Brahma's sphere. Brahmanda is not objective reality; it is Brahma's version of reality, his very own personal construction, his opinion of nature.

Prakriti is objective material reality. Brahmanda is subjective material reality. The former exists without the aid of Maya; the

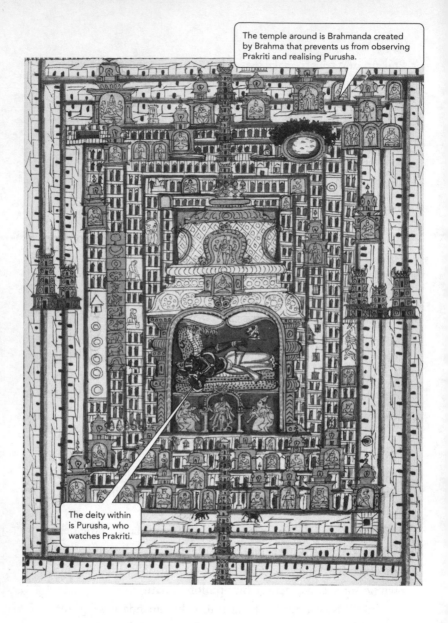

Mysore painting of the deity Ranganatha within the temple

latter is a product of Maya. Prakriti is the forest — in the forest, man is no different from other animals. Maya, however, makes man feel that he is superior to animal and that he is the master of the forest.

Objectively speaking, nature treats man no differently from any other living creature; we have been given a different set of strengths, and cunning, to survive. Subjectively speaking, however, man is different from all other living creatures — he can imagine, and this gives him the right to domesticate nature and create culture. Culture, the world imagined and constructed by man, with the aid of Maya, is Brahmanda.

Without Maya, man would be at the mercy of nature; with Maya, man is able to dominate nature and establish culture. Maya thus elevates man from being an animal. Life is no longer about survival alone; it is about meaning. The quest for meaning provokes man into action or karma, from the root 'Kri'(to do). In the quest for meaning, man creates society. Brahma thus becomes creator.

WHEN VISHNU IS IN DEEP slumber, he is not aware of Prakriti. That does not mean nature does not exist. It is simply not sensed. This state is described as Yoga-nidra. It is a state similar to when we are in deep slumber; we do not remember our name or anything about our life or our world. From a practical standpoint, our subjective reality does not exist. Subjective reality or Brahmanda is reborn only when we awaken, when the serpent Sesha transforms into Adi.

When awake, Vishnu observes nature just like Brahma. But unlike Brahma, he is not intimidated by Prakriti. Vishnu experiences no fear. He does not need a measuring scale to

South Indian painting of Vishnu and his consort, Yoga-maya

appreciate Prakriti. He sees Prakriti for what she is, without the aid of Maya, because he knows he is brahman. Brahma depends on Maya to survive Prakriti; Vishnu does not. Brahma is thus a slave of Maya while Vishnu is her master. Brahma needs to construct a subjective reality to make sense of existence, while Vishnu has no such need.

For Brahma, Maya is Maha-maya; he is under her spell. For Vishnu, Maya is Yoga-maya; she is under his command. That is why Vishnu is called Mayin, the great deluder.

Vishnu can, if he wishes, choose to engage with Maya. When he does, he takes the form of an avatar. For example, he can become Ram or Krishna. Both Ram and Krishna experience birth and death, like all human beings, but being realised souls, they are not afraid of Maya. Both know they are Vishnu; their identity is not dependent on any measuring scale or subjective reality.

Vishnu thus has a threefold relationship with Maya. As Narayana, he is ignorant of Maya. As Vishnu he is aware of Maya but chooses not to be under her spell, and as Vishnu's avatars, like Ram and Krishna, he willingly submits to Maya, engages with subjective realities, but is never dependent on her.

By engaging with Maya, Vishnu makes himself accessible to Brahma. As Ram and Krishna, he brings joy and breaks hearts, he participates in worldly affairs, seduces, fights, draws the jiva-atma towards him. The tangible world is the ranga-bhoomi or playground where one encounters spiritual reality. In the tangible world, Vishnu is both Mohan, the deluder, as well as Mohini, the enchantress.

Brahma blesses Suka-muni as he shared his wisdom with the world and encouraged everyone to realise infinity through Krishna.

The parrot-head indicates he shared with humanity exactly what his father said without any editing.

Calendar art showing Suka-muni, the parrot-headed son of Vyasa

The stories and images of Krishna aim to enchant the senses and overwhelm the emotions, thus giving value to subjective reality and worldly issues.

Temple image of Krishna as Man-mohan, the enchanter of the mind

THERE IS A STORY OF Vyasa's son, Suka. Suka refused to leave his mother's womb even after the stipulated ten lunar months had passed. His father begged him to come out and after twelve years of coaxing, Suka finally relented, not because he wanted to experience worldly life, but because he did not want to trouble his pregnant mother anymore.

Soon after birth, rather than step on earth, he rose skywards. He did not see the point of dealing with Maha-maya, and the subjective reality she would help him construct. While in his mother's womb, he had heard his father chant hymns of the Veda. He knew the difference between Maha-maya and Yoga-maya. He was not interested in creating his Brahmanda; he preferred the truth of Prakriti. He was not interested in finite truths; he wanted to experience infinity. This meant rising to the abode of Vishnu, and becoming one with him.

As Suka rose, his father cried out, 'Come back, come back.' But Suka refused to look back. It was then that Vyasa began describing Krishna's beauty. Vyasa said, 'His lotus feet, his curly hair, his winsome eyes, his mysterious smile, the peacock feather on his crown, the sandal paste marks on his long dark limbs, his broad chest with the curl of hair in the centre, his long legs draped in fine yellow silk, the garland of forest flowers round his neck, his dolphin-shaped earrings.'

So beautiful was the description that Suka stopped midway between the earth and the sky to hear his father. As the description progressed, he longed to see Krishna; somehow bondage did not seem so terrible anymore. It was enchanting. He realised that the only way to experience what he was hearing was to surrender to Maha-maya. Only in a limited, finite world of measurement could beauty be truly relished. Brahmanda

Temple wall sculpture from Belur, Karnataka, showing the many-headed Brahma

had its value. Only in subjective reality does Krishna manifest himself.

BRAHMA CREATED MANY SONS TO engage with Prakriti in order to realise brahman. He encouraged his sons to marry.

Marriage is a metaphysical metaphor for engagement with material reality. Marriage results in the construction of Brahmanda. Only through marriage can Brahma and his sons access Ram and Krishna, and through them discover Vishnu, and ultimately Narayana. Marriage is thus necessary for realising spiritual reality.

Amongst Brahma's many sons was one Narada. Narada refused to marry. He did not want anything to do with the material world. Like Suka, he preferred the realm of Narayana, when time and space do not exist, where Maya casts no spell. He went a step further; he encouraged Brahma's other sons to stay celibate like him. He did not see the point of engaging with Prakriti. He did not understand the point of constructing Brahmanda.

Many of Brahma's sons agreed with Narada. They also refused to marry. This happened several times, until an enraged Brahma cursed Narada, 'You will stay trapped in the material world until you appreciate the value of Maya.'

Narada went to Vishnu and asked him the meaning of Maya. In response, Vishnu said, 'I will explain after you quench my thirst. Go fetch me some water.'

Narada went to a river to fetch water. But as he was collecting the water, he saw a beautiful girl. He was so drawn to her that he followed her to her village and asked her father for her hand in marriage. The father agreed and the two got married. Before

Popular modern images of Narada with his lute

long, Narada was a father and then grandfather and then great grandfather. Narada felt content. Suddenly one day, it rained. And the rains refused to stop. The river swelled and broke its banks. Water rushed into Narada's house, and to his horror, swept away his wife, his children, his grandchildren and his great grandchildren. He screamed and shouted for help as the water dragged him under. Suddenly he was pulled up. He found himself in Vaikuntha beside Vishnu.

'Narada,' said Vishnu, 'where is my water? I am still thirsty.' Narada did not understand. Where was his family, his wife's village, the river?

'Where does this pain and suffering come from, Narada?' asked Vishnu with a smile. 'I thought you had full knowledge of Maya before you set out to fetch water for me.'

Narada bowed his head in realisation. He knew Maya but had never experienced Maya. Brahma was encouraging his sons to marry so that they could experience Maya. Knowledge of Maya is not experience of Maya. Unless one experiences Maya, one will not be able to empathise with those who are trapped in Maya.

Said Vishnu, 'You knew all about measuring scales and subjective realities. Yet you forgot all about them as soon as you experienced material pleasure — home, family, children, and village. Your understanding of Maya and Brahmanda could have helped you in the tumult of pleasure and pain, but it did not. Such is the spell of Maya. Now that you have experienced Maya, I want you to go and meet people, shake up their measuring scales, challenge their subjective realities, until they realise that the only way out of Maya is seeking answers outside material reality. I want you to provoke them into following the spiritual path.'

That is why Narada is renowned in Hindu mythology as a

A woodblock print from Bengal showing Krishna being weighed

trouble-maker. He disturbs the equilibrium of a happy material life, spreads turmoil through comparison and gossip. Once, Narada came to Krishna's house. Krishna's wives offered him a gift. 'I want you to give me Krishna,' said Narada. The wives were shocked by the request and naturally reluctant, but they could not go back on their promise. 'Then, in that case, offer me something that is equal to Krishna in weight.' A measuring balance was brought and Krishna was made to sit on one pan. On the other pan, one of the wives, Satyabhama, placed all the gold she possessed. Despite the vast quantity of gold, Krishna's pan remained lower, revealing that there is more to life than wealth. Then another of Krishna's wives, Rukmini, placed a sprig of the tulsi plant from her courtyard on top of the gold. It was the symbol of a devotee's love for Krishna. Instantly, Krishna's pan rose up, thus revealing that what matters more in life is not possession but affection. A person who is loved is always happier than a person with wealth. Thus, Narada's mischief led to wisdom even in Krishna's household.

Whenever Narada arrives on the scene, he does two things: he ignites a conflict and then chants 'Narayana, Narayana.' Conflict stems from things material and measurable, hence in the realm of Maya. Most people get embroiled in the conflict and pay no regard to the chant. The few who do listen to the chant surrender to a power that is indifferent to Maya: Narayana. This results in peace, realisation of brahman and entry into Vishnu's paradise, Vaikuntha.

IN THE MANY TALES OF mythology, Brahma never makes the journey out of Brahmanda into Vaikuntha. He convinces himself

Tulsi plants growing in a courtyard

that his subjective reality is objective reality. He ends up trying to control the world. Rather than looking beyond pleasure and pain, he works towards enhancing pleasure and reducing pain. He gets trapped in his own delusion. The material world stops being a medium, it becomes the destination. Brahma spends all his life securing his own version of reality. He does everything in his power to defend his measuring scale.

Brahma forgets Brahmanda is his creation. He forgets Maya is also his creation. He forgets Prakriti is his mother. Instead he seeks to control reality, dominate her, and make her dance to his whims. But Prakriti cannot be controlled by Brahma. The story goes that Brahma tries to get Shatarupa to dance to his whims. In other words, he tries to establish his control over Brahmanda. But the goddess runs away.

Brahma pursues her, desperate to possess and control her. It is a futile effort that he refuses to abandon. This Brahma, who chases Brahmanda, under the spell of Maya, is the unenlightened man, who seeks control over material reality, who seeks to dominate the world around him, seeks to make it function according to his whims. This is Brahma, the creator of all measuring scales and subjective realities, who is never worshipped.

In his obsession, Brahma sprouts many heads. The many heads of Brahma represent the gradual crumpling of human consciousness as it becomes increasingly contaminated by prejudices and conditioning. Finally, Brahma sprouts the fifth head, his own imaginary understanding of who he is. This is Brahma's self-image. It makes him demand significance in the world that he has created. Sometimes called the ego, this fifth head of Brahma is destroyed by Shiva.

Stone image showing Shiva and Vishnu merged into one,
a form known as Hara-Hari

SHIVA REJECTS BRAHMA'S INFATUATION WITH material reality and beheads him. Shiva is therefore called Kapalika, the beheader. Shiva is Bhairava, the conqueror of fear. He liberates Brahma from fear. But he does not stop there. He reverses the process started by the blooming of the lotus from Vishnu's navel.

Without his head, Brahma stops seeing nature. There is no imagination, no measuring scale, no subjective reality. There is no karma. There is no growth. There is nothing. There is a return to the dreamless slumber of Narayana. There is Sesha, zero. A return to entropy! No movement, only stillness. No sound, only silence.

Brahma, Vishnu and Shiva are the three aspects of spiritual reality. These three aspects of the spiritual engage with material reality in three different ways. Brahma is spiritual reality trying to find himself through material reality. Brahma creates measuring scales and subjective realities in his quest of self-realisation but ends up getting attached to it. Vishnu facilitates Brahma's liberation by celebrating the material world while Shiva facilitates Brahma's liberation by rejecting the material world.

Vishnu's way is called pravritti-marga or outward-looking path while Shiva's way is called nivritti-marga or the inward-looking path. Vishnu plays with Maya, without getting overwhelmed by her, while Shiva rejects her totally. Vishnu is therefore a more worldly form of the divine, a king and a warrior and a lover, while Shiva is a more monastic form of the divine, a hermit, who shuts his eyes to all things worldly.

Shiva shuts his eyes to the material world. He refuses to engage with Prakriti. In mythological narratives, he withholds all heat inside his being so that he becomes a pillar of fire. Around

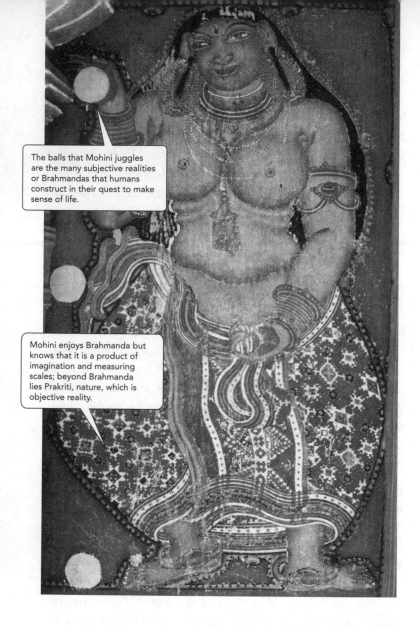

A Kerala mural of Vishnu as the voluptuous Mohini

him nothing moves or flows. Water becomes snow. All things become still. The world ceases to be. When Kama, the god of love, tries to strike an arrow of desire in his direction, he opens his third eye, releases a missile of fire and reduces Kama to ashes.

Shiva needs to open his eyes to material reality. He needs to be seduced. And so, Vishnu takes the form of an enchantress. He becomes Mohini and dances before Shiva. Shiva is compelled to open his eyes and look at Mohini. He recognises Mohini is Vishnu. She is spiritual reality cloaked in material reality. She is Vishnu playing with Prakriti and Maya. She is Vishnu in full control of time and space and subjective realities. Immersed in brahman, she is inviting spiritual reality to enter her playground, rangabhoomi, and join the game of material reality, the leela.

2
MATSYA'S SECRET
Only humans can empathise,
and exploit

The right line represents intellectual growth.

The left line represents emotional growth.

Vishnu's mark is always vertical, unlike Shiva's, which is always horizontal.

A saint with the mark of Vishnu

The white cup is created by a union of intellectual and emotional growth.

The white cup of spirituality always contains the red line of material growth.

Image of a temple gate

The sacred mark of Vishnu is always worn on the forehead, perhaps to draw attention to the one thing that distinguishes humans from animals: the larger brain.

The larger brain, especially the frontal brain, enables humans to imagine. Imagination allows us to conjure up a better world where we are not at the mercy of the elements. Imagination inspires us. We are driven to realise what we imagine. We inquire about the elements, and means to control it or improve upon it. We work towards creating technologies that will empower us to look beyond survival. In other words, it is this larger brain that compels us to create culture.

This larger brain transforms Pashu or animal into Purusha or human. It creates Brahma who seeks brahman. The larger brain is the physical manifestation of spiritual reality. It is born of Vishnu so that we can realise Vishnu.

Because humans have manas, the ability to imagine, humans are called Manavas. The first human is called Manu. The first story in the lore of Vishnu tells us how Vishnu engages with Manu in the form of a fish.

While Manu is performing his ablutions in a river, a fish approaches him and says, 'Save me from the big fish, and one day I will save you.' This request of the fish seems insignificant until one is informed that, in Hindu mythology, the phrase 'big fish eating small fish' refers to matsya nyaya, or the law of the fishes, which is jungle law.

That Vishnu first takes the form of a fish to engage with humankind is no coincidence. It is a deliberate attempt to draw attention to the jungle law — a law that only humans can overturn.

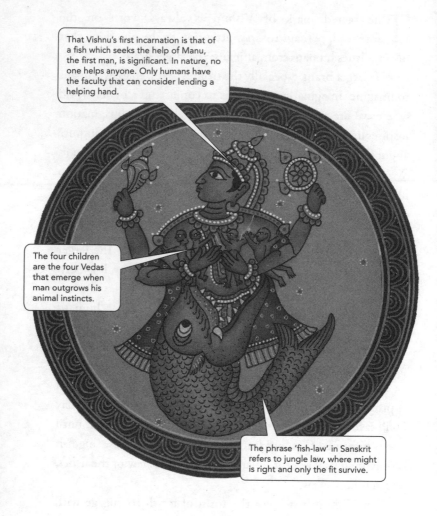

Mysore painting of Vishnu's fish incarnation

In the jungle, there are no rules. Only the fit survive and might is right. Might here does not mean physical strength, it also means intellectual strength. One can use one's strength and cunning in any way to survive. There is no right or wrong, no appropriate or inappropriate conduct. Anything goes as one fends for oneself. A goat is allowed to chomp on tender fresh grass. A lion is allowed to eat the goat. A wounded lion is abandoned and left to fend for itself. A hawk is allowed to swoop down and eat a snake that is just about to lay its eggs. A hyena is allowed to attack a doe in the middle of childbirth. Humans may judge animals as being cruel and insensitive, but animals do not see themselves this way. All their actions are driven by the need to survive. They do not judge the appropriateness of their actions. In fact they do not judge at all, because they cannot.

Of all living creatures, only humans can imagine a world where might is not right. Where the tiger and the goat live in harmony, where the hawk and serpent are friends. From this imagination comes the notion of heaven — the paradise of perfection. Desire to create this paradise of perfection provokes man into creating culture.

Manu does what no other creature can do. He responds to the cry of the little fish, collects it in the palm of his hand and puts it in a small pot. In other words, Manu interferes with nature. This interference has its roots in empathy. Manu feels the fear of the little fish and does something to allay it. The presence of Manu transforms nature. The little pot in which the fish is kept represents culture, a man-made creation, where the little fish is safe from the big fish.

It is this emotion and action that enables man to create society, a world where jungle law is challenged, where the mighty

Mysore painting of Matsya, Vishnu's first incarnation

take care of the meek, where the weak are given opportunities by the strong. The thought that creates this secure world is called dharma, from the root 'Dhr' which means 'to make secure' or 'to bind'.

Dharma thus is an artificial construct. One can argue that Dharma is what is natural to man. In overturning matsya nyaya lies purusha-artha, the validation of human existence. That is why humans were created. So long as we follow jungle law, we are pashu or animals. Only when we rise above it and start establishing dharma do we become purusha or human.

MANU'S WATER POT THAT CONTAINS the fish is Manu's property, his to give to the fish. The notion of property reminds us that, fundamentally, Manu is still animal and relies on the notion of territory.

In nature, animals have territory. They mark it by spraying their urine. This territory ensures the animal has enough to eat. The territory also ensures that the animal has exclusive rights on a mate, so that it can reproduce and create the next generation. Territory is critical to the survival of the beast. If another animal seeks access to this territory, it has to contend with the previous master. And in keeping with the laws of the jungle, the contention is usually violent.

But Manu's notion of property is quite different from an animal's notion of territory. Territory cannot be inherited. Territory cannot be bequeathed. One has to fight for territory. No rules and laws protect it. Without territory, animals will not survive.

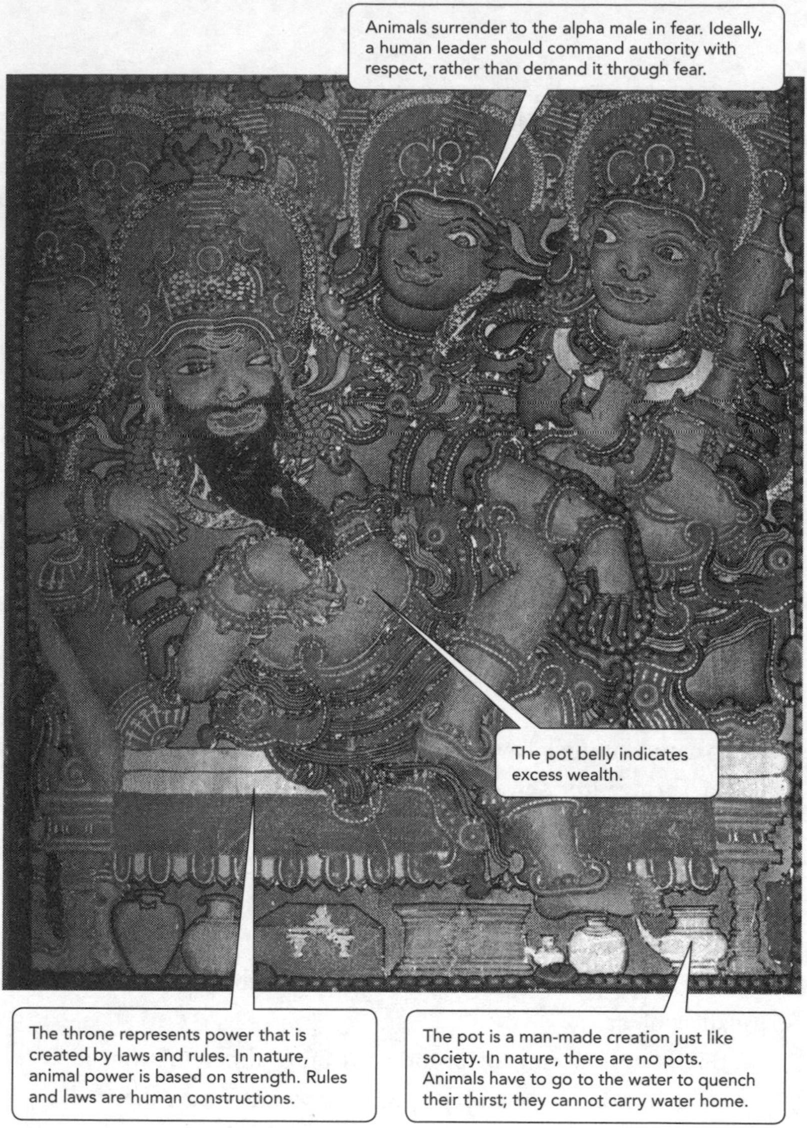

Kerala mural of a king

Human property is not just about need. At one extreme, human property is based on compassion — to provide for more and more people, even unrelated people, like the fish, for example, that Manu provides for. This compassion stems from empathy, imagination of other people's fear. At the other extreme, human property is based on greed — to hoard more and more for oneself, even when there is no immediate need. This greed stems from fear, an imagination of scarcity that is unique to humans. In greed, we exploit the earth's resources. We also exploit fellow human beings. Thus property has its roots in imagination. When the imagination leads to empathy, property becomes inclusive; this is dharma. When the imagination amplifies fear and supports exploitation, property becomes exclusive; this is adharma.

Animals give up territory only when forced to but humans have the ability to give up property voluntarily. This is made explicit in the *Ramayana*, an epic which tells the story of Ram, a form of Vishnu that walked the earth.

In the *Ramayana*, the Rakshasa-king Ravana drives his half-brother Kubera, the Yaksha-king, out of Lanka and claims the island-city as his own. Ram, however, is more than willing to let his brother, Bharata, become king of his kingdom, Ayodhya. When asked by his father to give up his claim to the throne in favour of his younger brother, Ram does so willingly, without hesitation or regret. Ram is therefore identified with dharma while Ravana is identified with adharma. Ram realises his human potential, which makes him God, Bhagavan, worthy of worship. Ravana fails to realise his human potential, which makes him Rakshasa, a demon, unworthy of respect.

Sugriva combats Vali's strength with cunning by befriending Ram of Ayodhya, a human.

Vali is stronger than Sugriva but is killed by an arrow shot by Ram from behind a bush.

Mysore painting showing Vali and Sugriva fighting

THE FISH GROWS IN SIZE and so Manu transfers it from a small pot to a bigger pot. The fish keeps getting bigger and to accommodate it, out of compassion for the poor creature, Manu keeps providing it with bigger and bigger pots.

In the *Ramayana*, two monkeys fight over territory, the kingdom of Kishkinda. They are two brothers, Vali and Sugriva, the sons of Riksha. The two brothers are supposed to share the kingdom, but following a misunderstanding, Vali drives his brother Sugriva out of the kingdom. Vali even forcibly claims Sugriva's wife, Ruma, for himself. When Vishnu descends on earth as Ram, he interferes in this fight between the alpha male, Vali, and the contender, Sugriva. While the two brothers fight, Ram shoots an arrow from behind a bush and strikes Vali dead. Vali protests. 'This is against dharma,' he says. Ram argues that a monkey who lives by the law of the jungle must die by the law of the jungle.

Vali has no right to quote the rules of dharma because dharma is based on sharing property, on inclusion not exclusion. Vali behaved like an animal when he refused to share his kingdom and when he forcibly deprived his brother of the kingdom and his wife; Sugriva was therefore entitled to use cunning to deprive his brother of his life. The law of the jungle is a valid option in the realm of adharma.

With Vali dead, Sugriva becomes lord of Kishkinda. Ram now demands that Sugriva follow dharma and appoint Vali's son, Angad, as his heir. In the animal world, when the alpha male takes over, it kills the children of the overthrown leader. Dharma must, however, be rooted in compassion. Ram demands Sugriva change: if Vali followed matsya nyaya, Sugriva must follow dharma. Vali saw Kishkinda as territory and refused to share;

Mughal painting showing Shibi saving a dove from a hawk

Sugriva must see Kishkinda as property and pass it on to his erstwhile rival's son. Thus the pot of Ram, containing dharma, once limited to Ayodhya, now expands to include Kishkinda.

THE DESIRE FOR THE LARGER pot can also indicate a lack of sensitivity and a lack of contentment. As more of the forest is domesticated and turned into fields to provide for human society, more and more of nature is destroyed for culture. Human laws tend to include some and exclude some and in doing so push nature to its limits. This is evident in the following story from the *Mahabharata*.

A king called Shibi, in compassion, rescues a dove being chased by a hawk. The hawk asks the king, 'What will I eat now?' The king suggests he eat another dove. The hawk retorts, 'So that you can indulge your compassion for this dove, you are willing to sacrifice another dove. Is that fair?' The king then asks the hawk to eat a rat or a serpent. 'Why should they die so that the dove can live?' This question has no answer.

In being kind to the dove, the king is being cruel to the hawk. The king has included the dove but excluded the hawk. Why should the dove be saved? Why should the hawk be made to starve? These questions, which have no answers, challenge the human construct of society.

Man creates society as he pursues his imagination of paradise, a place where all creatures are safe. However, in the process, he creates a world where some are more safe than others. Human society invariably favours a few over others. Culture is thus always imperfect. Vishnu lore always draws attention to this truism, for Vishnu is a worldly god and knows that seeking

Balarama, like his brother Krishna, wears fabric made of cotton and silk. To get cotton one needs to farm. To establish a farm one has to destroy a forest. To get silk one needs to kill silkworms to claim their cocoon. Thus culture favours humans at the cost of nature.

Mysore painting of Balarama

Balarama's plough indicates his association with farming activities.

The dragging of Yamuna is suggestive of canal-building, a violent activity that results in the destruction of riverbanks but irrigates fields and orchards.

Pahari miniature showing Balarama and Yamuna

answers by controlling material reality will never be satisfactory.

In the *Mahabharata*, the Pandavas seek to build a city in the forest given to them by their uncle. The only way to do this is by burning down the forest. Vishnu in the form of Krishna encourages them to do so. As the forest burns, the birds and the beasts of the forest try to run away to save themselves only to be shot down by arrows released by the Pandavas at the behest of Krishna. This reeks of cruelty until one realises that until the forest is burnt, a field cannot be established. Culture is built on the destruction of a natural ecosystem.

In the *Bhagavata Purana*, Krishna's elder brother, Balarama, also a form of Vishnu, wants the river Yamuna to come to him so that he can bathe without making the effort to go to the river. The river-goddess refuses to come to him. Enraged, Balarama grabs the river-goddess by her hair and forces her to come to him. In some versions, he uses his plough to hook her side and bring her to where he is. The act is described in extremely violent terms, for material reality has been subjugated with force against her will. The story alludes to the practice of canal irrigation, which is not natural. It entails the destruction of riverbanks and with it the destruction of many animals that may have depended on an intact riverbank for their survival.

Manu's motivation may be noble, but it includes only the fish in the pot, not the other fishes outside. Thus, what begins as empathy for one ends up becoming rather exclusive — lack of empathy for the rest.

HUMANS CAN NEVER INCLUDE EVERYBODY. Plants and animals are excluded if they do not serve the needs of society.

Stone carving of fish

Crops are included, weeds are not. Domesticated animals are welcomed but wild animals are shunned. People whose points of view align with ours are included; the rest are excluded. Society will always exclude somebody. And this exclusion eventually claims a huge price.

So the fish gets bigger and bigger, utilising all the resources provided by Manu, and Manu keeps transferring it to bigger pots to satisfy its ever-growing needs. At no point does Manu think the fish can fend for itself and so he does not bother to throw the fish back into the sea. At no point does the fish think it can fend for itself and ask Manu to throw it back into the sea. The fish in the pot gradually becomes dependent on Manu and displays no desire to be independent. Eventually the fish has to be put in a pond, then a larger pond, then a lake and finally a river. A point comes in the story when dark clouds gather overhead and it rains relentlessly. The sea begins to swell and swallow the earth. It is Pralaya, death of the world.

This is what happens when human society becomes so focussed on itself that it loses touch with the rest of nature, when culture expands at the cost of everything else, when the needs of culture override the needs of nature. Eventually something will snap. Nature will strike back.

At first Manu wonders why he is suffering even though he spent his life doing a noble deed: caring for the small fish. He blames the rain and curses the sea. But then realisation dawns.

This is not explicitly stated in the scriptures as Manu is the reader of the tale. Manu is all of humanity. This wisdom has to be figured out by the story-listener, not communicated by the story-teller.

Manu realises that his obsession with the small fish is the

Miniature painting showing Vishnu killing Panchajana, the conch-shell demon

Miniature painting of Manu's ship being towed by the horned fish

cause of the great calamity. This obsession made him insensitive to the fact that the fish had grown and could take care of itself. He became insensitive to the consequences of his action on the rest of the world. Every action has a reaction that one is bound to experience. This is the law of karma. Just as society is created by an act of compassion, when Manu saves the fish, society is destroyed when the compassion becomes exclusive, and fails to include all of nature. When Manu realises this, he takes responsibility for his role in Pralaya. It is then that the fish reappears before Manu. This time, the fish has a horn on his forehead.

WHY A HORN ON HIS forehead? Is it to direct Manu towards his larger brain, that source of imagination, that root of empathy and exploitation? The horn is very much like the vertical mark of Vishnu, reminding Manu that life is about growth. Manu grew from animal to human when he saved the fish; but he was unable to make the move from human to divine when he focused exclusively on the fish, and became too insensitive to include the rest. While there was material growth, indicated by the larger pots, there was no emotional and intellectual growth to realise that he has to expand his vision to include all.

The horned fish guides Manu to build a boat, much like the Biblical Noah's ark. The fish asks Manu to tie the boat to his horn using the serpent Adi-Ananta-Sesha. The fish then tows the ship to safety to Mount Meru, the centre of the world. When the waters recede, an enlightened Manu saved by the fish and its horn starts the world anew.

Photograph of Shalagrama stones, considered a form of Vishnu

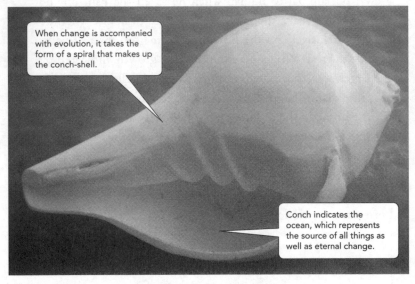

Photograph of a conch-shell

IN SOME VERSIONS OF The story, a demon called Panchajana steals the Veda and hides at the bottom of the sea as Pralaya claims the earth. Vishnu in the form of a fish defeats the demons, rescues the Vedas and hands them over to Manu. Having killed the demon, Vishnu turns the conch-shell in which the demon had hidden into a trumpet called Panchajanya. This Vishnu blows so that everyone hears the secret of the Veda.

And what is this secret? In nature, all plants and animals move cyclically and predictably. They have no choice but to stay within this wheel. But humans have the power to break this cycle, turn the wheel into a spiral that winds outwards and inwards. The break in trajectory happens when humans break free from fear, empathise, follow dharma and transcend animal instincts to realise divinity.

The spirals of the conch-shell, sacred to Vishnu, are reminders of this unique human possibility.

3
KURMA'S SECRET
Wealth eludes the insecure

Kerala mural showing Lakshmi in the arms of Vishnu

Lakshmi is the goddess of wealth. She is described as dressed in red, bedecked with gold, seated on a lotus, holding a pot overflowing with grain and gold. Everyone worships her as she provides sustenance to all beings. She is the food that we eat, the clothes that we wear, the house that we live in. Without her, we cannot survive.

Lakshmi does not discriminate. A bowl of rice will satisfy a saint and a sinner. A blanket will provide the same warmth to a king or a beggar. A house will equally shelter a man or a woman.

But Lakshmi is restless. She never stays in one place for long. And no one knows what makes her move. Some describe her as cockeyed; one may think she is going in one direction but then she ends up going somewhere else.

Since wealth in its most primal form, metal and plants, comes from under the ground, Lakshmi is described in scriptures as Patala-Nivasini, she who lives in Patala. 'Pa' means foot and 'tala' means below. Lakshmi is thus the resident of subterranean realms. This is the realm of the Asuras.

Asuras are the grandchildren of Brahma. Their father is Kashyapa and their mother is Diti. For humans, who seek access to wealth, Asuras are demons who withhold Lakshmi under the earth. Humans worship Devas who they declare as gods because they help release Lakshmi and draw her to the surface out of her subterranean prison. Devas are the half-brothers of the Asuras. They have the same grandfather, Brahma, and the same father, Kashyapa, but a different mother, Aditi.

The leader of the Devas is Indra, who strikes clouds and brings rain. He is both sky-god and rain-god. His brothers are Agni, the fire-god, who sits on the ground; Vayu, the wind-god, who moves between the earth and the sky; Surya and Chandra,

Stone image of Kubera, king of Yakshas

Stone image of a Yaksha with a Yakshini

the sun-god and the moon-god, who reside in the sky. His guru is Brihaspati, lord of the planet Jupiter, associated with rationality and mathematics.

Brihaspati performs a yagna for Indra, giving him the power to draw Lakshmi from under the earth. Agni and Vayu melt rocks and release metal. The wind and the sun and the rain draw plants from under the earth.

Stories of Devas killing Asuras are thus stories of Lakshmi's release from subterranean confinement. That is why the acts of mining, hunting, fishing, farming and harvesting, which generate wealth, are so violent. Unless the rock is broken, metal cannot be released. Unless the grain is threshed, grain will not be released. In other words, for Lakshmi to be obtained, Asuras need to be killed.

For Indra, Lakshmi is Sachi, his wife. But for Asuras, she is Pulomi, daughter of Puloman, their king. She is also Bhargavi, daughter of their guru, Bhrigu, also known as Shukra, lord of the planet Venus, associated with intuition and creativity. Considering the close association of Lakshmi and the Asuras, it is not surprising that the abode of Asuras is Hiranyapura, or the city of gold.

Lakshmi is also associated with other 'demonic' subterranean and wild creatures like Yakshas and Rakshasas. Yakshas live near water bodies and are visualised as misshapen beasts. The king of Yakshas is Kubera, who is sometimes described as a treasurer of the gods, hoarding wealth and keeping a count of every penny. Kubera built the golden city of Lanka, which was usurped by his brother, Ravana, king of the Rakshasas.

Wood carving of Indra, king of the Devas

When Lakshmi sits beside Indra as Sachi, Indra's city of Amravati, located above the sky, transforms into Swarga, or paradise. It houses Kalpataru, the wish-fulfilling tree, Kamadhenu, the wish-fulfilling cow, and Chintamani, the wish-fulfilling gem. All this wealth should make Indra, secure and happy. But it makes him insecure. He fears Sachi will leave his side and choose someone more worthy to be her husband.

King Sagara once performed the Ashwamedha yagna. This involved letting loose the royal horse and following it with one's army. All the land that the horse traversed unchallenged came under the king's rule. King Sagara was so powerful that no king dared stop his horse. As a result he was on his way to becoming Chakravarti, ruler of the circular horizon, meaning the ruler of the whole world. He would then be powerful enough to overthrow Indra. An insecure Indra stole the horse and hid it in the hermitage of a Rishi called Kapila. Sagara's sons found the horse and accused Kapila of theft. Kapila glanced at them so angrily that they all burst into flames. Having thus lost his sons, Sagara lost all interest in his yagna. And Indra felt safe.

Another time, a Rishi called Kandu was busy performing tapasya. This was a practice involving the control of the five senses so as to generate inner heat or tapa. With this tapa, Kandu would have the power to control nature, manipulate it to his whims. Indra feared that if Kandu was successful in his practice, he would overthrow him. To prevent such an eventuality, he sent an Apsara called Pramlocha to seduce Kandu. Pramlocha was successful in her quest. Such was the passion of her lovemaking that Kandu lost sense of time; a hundred years seemed like one night. When Kandu finally recovered his senses, he realised he had been beguiled by the nymph on Indra's instruction and he could

Cambodian temple carving showing Indra on elephants

do nothing about it.

Indra does not trust Sachi, because he does not trust himself, and he does not trust himself because he does not know himself. Like Brahma, he is not aware of spiritual reality. Thus he is plagued by ideas of impermanence and mortality.

To distract himself from his fears, Indra immerses himself in pleasure and becomes a hedonist. Sachi eventually runs away, not because she is attracted to another king or sage, but because she is repelled by Indra's behaviour.

Once, the Rishi Durvasa, known for his temper, offers Indra a garland of beautiful lotus flowers. But Indra, surrounded by damsels, and in a state of intoxication, takes the garland and simply tosses it on the floor, allowing it to be trampled by his elephant, Airavata. Enraged, Durvasa curses Indra, 'You will lose it all — the wish-fulfilling tree, the wish-fulfilling cow, and the wish-fulfilling gem. Lakshmi will slip out of this realm.' And that is precisely what happens.

In other stories, misfortune follows after Indra angers his guru, Brihaspati, with his insolence. One way or the other, Indra always loses his fortune, and he is always to blame for it, no one else.

With Lakshmi gone, a mortified Indra rushes to his father, Brahma. 'Help me bring her back,' he cries. But Brahma does not know how to help the Devas. He advises them to seek the help of Vishnu. And Vishnu says, 'The goddess has dissolved herself in the ocean of milk. Churn her out. Use the king of the mountains, Mandara, as the churning staff. And use the king of serpents, Vasuki, as the churning rope.' In other variants of

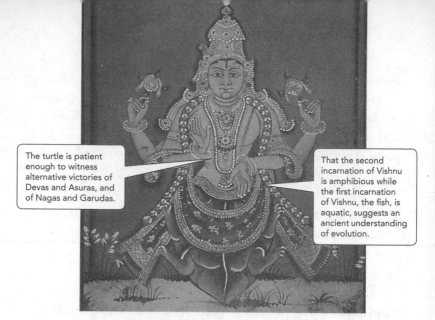

The turtle is patient enough to witness alternative victories of Devas and Asuras, and of Nagas and Garudas.

That the second incarnation of Vishnu is amphibious while the first incarnation of Vishnu, the fish, is aquatic, suggests an ancient understanding of evolution.

Mysore painting of Kurma, the turtle form of Vishnu

Temples dedicated to Kurma avatar are rare; one is located in Karnataka (Gavirangapura) and another in Andhra Pradesh (Srikurmam).

A rare image of Kurma worshipped in a temple at the village of Gavirangapura, Karnataka

this tale, the churning staff is Meru, the axis of space, and the churning rope is Adi-Ananta-Sesha, the serpent of time.

The Devas try to carry the king of the mountains, but Mandara is too heavy even for all of them put together. They try to drag out the king of serpents from the subterranean realms, but Vasuki refuses to budge. So they beg Vishnu to help. Vishnu tells his hawk, the mighty Garuda, to pick up the mountain and pull out the snake and bring them to the ocean of milk. 'But how will the spindle stay afloat. Mandara will surely sink to the bottom of the ocean,' cry the Devas. To their astonishment, they find a giant turtle called Kurma, rising up to the surface of the sea. It is none other than Vishnu. Garuda places Mandara on Kurma's back and then winds Vasuki around the mountain. The churn is ready.

The Devas start churning the ocean of milk. But they lack the strength to serve as the force and counterforce. Vishnu advises them, 'You need to take the help of your half-brothers, the Asuras. You hold the tail of Vasuki and serve as the force of the churn. Make the Asuras hold the neck of Vasuki and serve as the counterforce.'

Though born of the same father, the Devas and the Asuras hate each other. The Asuras feel Lakshmi belongs under the earth and the Devas feel she belongs above. But with her disappearance, both have no choice but to cooperate and bring her out. And so the Asuras join the Devas and agree to serve as the counterforce of the churn.

THE CHURNING STARTS IN EARNEST. When the Devas pull, the Asuras relax and when the Asuras pull, the Devas relax. By

Calendar image of Kurma, the turtle form of Vishnu

placing them as the force and counterforce, Vishnu successfully makes two opposing sides work towards a common goal.

But the exercise is not an easy one. It involves a great deal of time and a great deal of effort. The Devas and the Asuras have to work as never before.

Milk is a common metaphor in Hindu narratives. It represents the material world full of possibilities. But to get the best out of milk, it has to be churned. It has to be turned into butter and finally clarified to make ghee. The whole process involves a lot of effort. In Vishnu temples, Vishnu always demands butter and ghee, unlike Shiva who is content with raw unboiled milk, for Vishnu is the God who celebrates the best the material world has to offer, while Shiva is God who is indifferent to material reality. Lakshmi is the best that the material world has to offer. Vishnu celebrates her.

Eventually, as butter rises when milk is churned, the ocean of milk begins to spew out its many treasures. There is the flying horse, Ucchaishrava, and the white-skinned elephant with seven trunks, Airavata. There is the Parijata tree, another name for Kalpataru, and there is Kamadhenu and there is Chintamani, also known as Kaustubha. There is the nymph called Rambha and wine called Varuni.

All these are the treasures that once adorned Indra's Swarga. Significant amongst these are Rambha and Varuni, women and wine. It is these indulgences that cost Indra his fortune and yet the scriptures acknowledge that these are pleasures that are very much a part of worldly life. Ancient texts are not embarrassed by sensual pleasures. They appreciate their value but also warn of the dangers of overindulgence. Thus Indra's Swarga is a place where women dance and wine flows, and it is precisely these

Cambodian temple wall sculpture showing the churning of the ocean of milk

luxuries that make Indra lose his sensibility.

The horse and the elephant represent dharma, or righteous conduct. The tree, the cow and the gem represent artha, or wealth. The nymph and the wine represent kama or pleasure. Thus from the ocean came righteous conduct and wealth and pleasure. These are the gifts of the ocean. These are the gifts that announced the arrival of Lakshmi, the goddess of wealth.

As soon as Lakshmi rises, everyone gets excited. She is draped in a red sari, covered with jewels and seated on a lotus. In her hand is the Akshaya Patra, the vessel that is eternally overflowing with grain and gold. The Devas and the Asuras sing praises to this beautiful and enchanting goddess. White elephants that reside in the cardinal and ordinal directions rush to welcome her; they raise their trunks and sprinkle her with fragrant water.

Everyone waits with bated breath to see where Lakshmi will go. Will she be the wife of the Devas or the daughter of the Asuras? But to everyone's surprise, she moves towards Vishnu and garlands him, thereby declaring him her husband.

The Asuras want Lakshmi, so do the Devas, but Lakshmi wants Vishnu who does not yearn for her. This is significant. Why does Lakshmi choose Vishnu? Because Vishnu is enterprising — he designs the churn and gets enemies to work together. She also selects him because he is detached from the entire enterprise. He helps the Devas but does not seek the treasures the ocean has to offer.

Vishnu knows he is spiritual reality, brahman, infinite and immortal, and hence knows the truth about Lakshmi who is material reality. He does not derive any significance from her but knows she enables him to understand himself. Therefore he

North Indian miniature painting showing Lakshmi flanked by two elephants pouring water on her

A temple sculpture from Belur, Karnataka, showing Lakshmi seated on Vishnu's thigh

does not attempt to control her. Instead, he enjoys her whimsical nature. His knowledge of Lakshmi makes him smile.

In the *Ramayana*, Ram does not lose his composure when he is asked to leave the palace and live in the forest. He is as much at peace in the palace as he is in the forest. He does not derive his identity from material reality. This quality of Vishnu makes him attractive to Lakshmi. Vishnu is therefore called Shri-nivasa or Shri-vatsa, which means abode of Lakshmi. He is Lakshmi-vallabha or Lakshmi-kanta, which means the beloved of Lakshmi. He is Shri-natha or Thiru-pati, which means he who is the lord of Lakshmi. He does not chase her, but she always follows him.

In art, Vishnu is shown sleeping on the coils of the serpent Adi-Ananta-Sesha, who floats on the ocean of milk. Lakshmi sits at his feet, massaging his legs, demure and domesticated. This is totally unlike her character. Lakshmi is a flamboyant goddess who goes where she wills. Neither the Devas nor the Asuras, who fight to possess her, can control her. There is something about Vishnu that makes her willingly surrender her autonomy. He does not seek her and this is precisely why she wants to follow him and serve him. Vishnu is therefore Shrivatsa, the one whose abode is Lakshmi. Where he is, so is she.

LAKSHMI HAS A SISTER, ALAKSHMI. She is the goddess of strife. Whenever wealth enters a house, so does Lakshmi's sister, causing quarrels. Alakshmi is the chaff of the grain that is Lakshmi. Alakshmi is the pollutant that accompanies the metal that is Lakshmi. Alakshmi is the skin and seed that cannot be eaten of the juicy fruit pulp that is Lakshmi. The two always

Poster art from Bengal showing an owl seated beside Lakshmi

come together. So when Lakshmi rises from the ocean of milk, so does Alakshmi, in the form of Halahal, a terrible poison.

Black viscid scum fills the air with a putrid stench. Light disappears and the Devas and the Asuras choke as vile fumes envelope everything in sight. 'Save us,' they cry to Vishnu.

Vishnu immediately invokes Shiva, the God whose indifference enable him to accept all that which everyone rejects. Everyone accepts Lakshmi and yearns for the wonderful gifts that accompany her, but no one accepts Halahal. Someone has to accept Halahal, otherwise it will destroy the world. So Shiva is summoned and Shiva consumes Halahal in one gulp.

In some folk narratives, Alakshmi emerges from Halahal and demands she be given a husband. If Vishnu has accepted Lakshmi, someone must accept her. Since neither the Devas nor the Asuras want her, she is given to the only one who has no preferences or prejudices. Shiva!

Some scholars are of the opinion that Alakshmi represents wild and undomesticated Kali. Others believe that Alakshmi and Lakshmi together embody Prakriti. Lakshmi is the desirable aspect of nature, while Alakshmi is the undesirable aspect of nature. If Lakshmi is love, then Alakshmi is conflict. If Lakshmi is alluring nourishment, then Alakshmi is venomous pollution. One cannot exist without the other. The difference between the two is created by Maya. Vishnu does not see the difference. He embraces Lakshmi in her totality, with Alakshmi. He knows what is the place of Lakshmi and what is the place of Alakshmi. He knows that Alakshmi must never be ignored or disregarded.

WHAT DISTINGUISHES VISHNU FROM SHIVA is that Vishnu

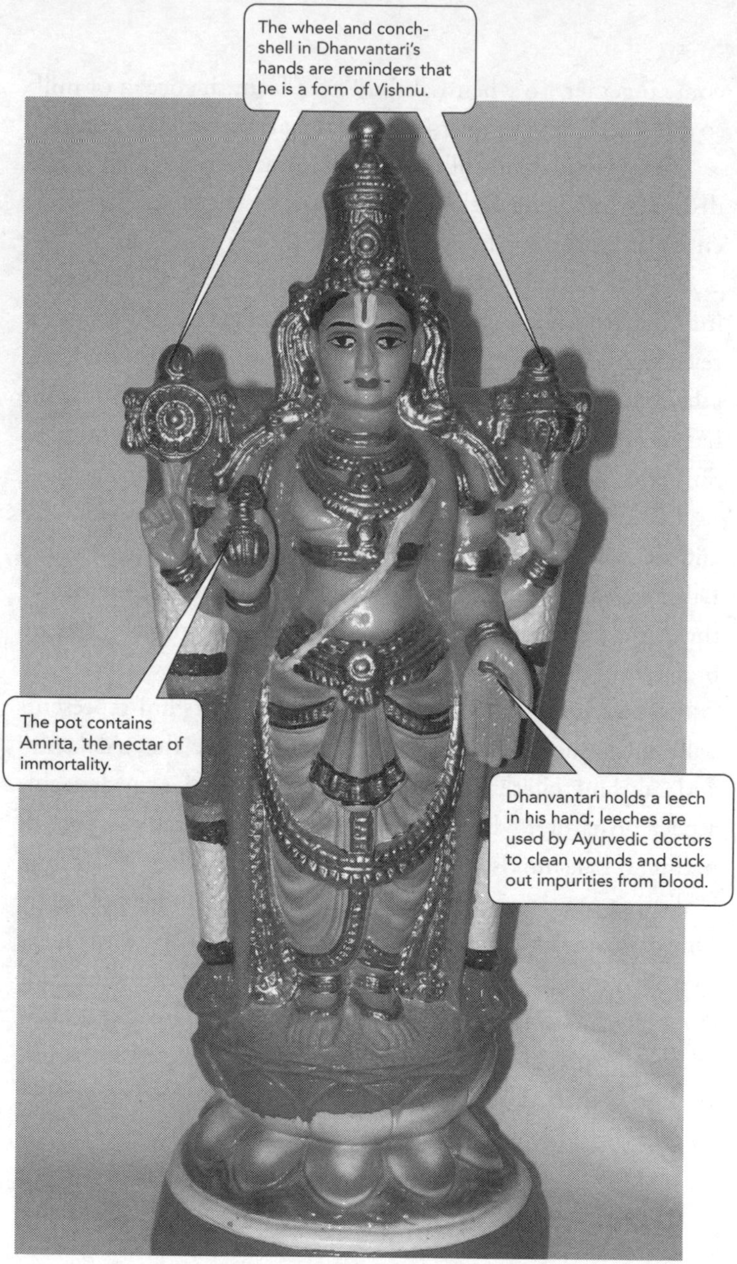

South Indian doll of Dhanvantari, god of medicine

is a very discerning form of God, unlike Shiva. Shiva takes no sides; he neither loves nor hates the Devas or the Asuras. By consuming Halahal, he saves both Devas and Asuras. Vishnu, by contrast, takes the side of the Devas and nowhere is this more evident than in the story of Amrita.

Amrita is the nectar of immortality. And it is the final treasure to emerge from the ocean of milk after Lakshmi and Halahal. It emerges from the sea in the arms of a deity called Dhanvantari, the god of health and healing. He is the god of Ayurveda, which is the traditional Indian medicine.

Dhanvantari is a form of Vishnu. Like Vishnu he holds a conch-shell trumpet and a wheel, but what distinguishes him from Vishnu is the pot of nectar in one hand and the leech that he holds in another. This leech is used by those who practise Ayurveda to drain pus from infected ulcers. Sometimes, instead of the bowl of Amrita, he is shown holding herbs in his hand or a pestle and mortar to make pastes and ointments.

Everybody wants Amrita, the nectar of immortality. All the children of Brahma, whether they are 'gods' or 'demons', fear death. Everyone wants to live forever. So both the Devas and the Asuras rush to grab the pot of nectar. The partnership that helped the churning collapses. A fight ensues, each one claiming full right over the nectar. Everyone agrees that all those who churned the ocean have a right to the nectar, but who shall drink first? The Devas and the Asuras do not trust each other.

Vishnu then takes the form of Mohini and appears before the Devas and the Asuras. She is so beautiful that everyone is overwhelmed with desire. It is said that Shiva, having consumed Halahal, was about to retreat to his mountainous abode when he sees Mohini. He is so enchanted by her beauty that he embraces

Poster art of Aiyappa, or Hari-Hara-Suta, the son of
Vishnu and Shiva, worshipped in Kerala

her. From that union of Shiva and Mohini is born Hari-Hara-Suta, the son of Vishnu and Shiva, a child who possesses the ascetic qualities of Shiva, hence refuses to marry, as well as the warrior qualities of Vishnu, hence is ever-willing to defend society. In Tamil Nadu, this warrior-ascetic is called Aiyanar. In Kerala, he is Manikantha or Sastha or Aiyappa, whose shrine is built atop the Sabari hill. No women are allowed to this shrine. And men have to practise weeks of celibacy and simplicity to gain access there.

Mohini is so enchanting that, for a moment, everyone forgets the nectar. She speaks in a melodious voice. 'May I distribute the nectar.' No one can say no to so delightful a creature.

The pot of nectar is given to the enchantress and all the Devas and the Asuras sit down awaiting their turn. Mohini sails amongst them, smiling invitingly, her eyes twinkling, pouring Amrita down their throats.

Suddenly, the Asuras notice that Mohini is pouring the Amrita down the throats of only the Devas. Nothing is being given to the Asuras. They realise there is mischief afoot. They are being tricked by the damsel. They raise their weapons and rush towards Mohini, determined to snatch the pot of nectar once again. But now all the Devas have been nourished with Amrita; they are immortal. They run to Mohini's rescue. A great battle follows. The weapons of the Asuras have no effect on the Devas and with great ease the Devas are able to defeat the Asuras.

With the Asuras dead, the Devas, now unafraid of death, rise to their celestial abode, Amravati, with all the wonderful treasures that had emerged from the ocean of milk.

Mohini carrying the pot of Amrita.

Asuras craving for Amrita but distracted by Mohini.

Devas craving for Amrita but distracted by Mohini.

South Indian stone carving showing Mohini, the female form of Vishnu

AT FIRST GLANCE, THIS STORY of how Mohini tricks the Asuras and gives the Amrita to the Devas seems like a trickster story. The demons are duped by a damsel. Since the Asuras are villains, one is told, they deserve being cheated so. But this is a simplistic and incorrect understanding of the tale.

One must remember that the Devas and the Asuras are half-brothers, children of Brahma who, like Vishnu, is a form of God. English translations that equate Asuras with demons are more judgmental than descriptive. No one is sure what is the 'villainous' deeds for which the Asuras are condemned so. Yet, one is quick to visualise them as horrible monstrous ogres. And this impatient conclusion prevents one from seeing the big picture.

The big picture is that while the Devas do not die, the Asuras are also blessed with a power that enables them to survive death. When killed in battle, they can be resurrected, because their guru, Shukra, son of Bhrigu, has access to the secret occult lore known as Sanjivani Vidya. And Shukra obtained this lore from Shiva, the indifferent ascetic.

If Brahma, the creator, is equally passionate about the Devas and the Asuras, Shiva in his role of destroyer is equally indifferent to both the Devas and the Asuras. So both Brahma and Shiva neutralise each other, giving equal boons to both the Devas and the Asuras. As a result there is no motion in the world, no movement, no change, no happening. The only way to create motion is to create a gradient of power, generate opposition between two equal forces so that they serve as the force and counterforce of a churn. Vishnu, in his role as preserver, spurs this motion in the cosmos by creating an imbalance of power, by giving Amrita to the Devas and denying it to the Asuras.

Poster art showing Mohini favouring Devas

The Devas always kill the Asuras and take Lakshmi to Swarga. Sometimes they do this on their own and sometimes with a little help from Vishnu. However, thanks to Indra's insecurity, and consequential hedonism, they cannot hold on to Lakshmi for long. She goes away and, to get her back, the Asuras are needed once more. The resurrection of Asuras by Sanjivani Vidya ensures the fertility of the land is restored every year and the crops rise every year, despite the 'killing' during the last harvest. Every time the Asuras rise, the battle of the Devas and Asuras starts anew. The Asuras die, Lakshmi is gathered by the Devas and the cycle begins anew.

Both Devas and Asuras are critical to ensure the movement of Lakshmi. Devas distribute her and Asuras create her. That is why, in yagnas, offerings are made to Suras, which means Devas who consumed Amrita, and to the Asuras, who were denied Amrita. Vishnu does not seek the absolute and eternal defeat of the Asuras. For if that happens, the churning will stop and the world will come to an end.

CONFLICT BETWEEN TWO FORCES IS a recurring theme in Hindu mythology. One conflict is that between material and spiritual reality, between the hermit and the nymph, between Shiva and Mohini. The other is within material reality, between the Devas and the Asuras.

The conflict within material reality, presided over by Vishnu, also manifests as the conflict between the Nagas and Garuda, the serpents and the king of the hawks, both being sacred to Vishnu.

Like the Asuras, serpents live under the ground, and like the

South Indian painting of Garuda

city of the Asuras, the city of the Nagas, Bhogavati, is made of gold and gems. Like the Devas, the hawk flies in the sky above. Like Asuras and Devas, the serpents and the king of the hawks are half-brothers, children of Brahma, of two wives.

Brahma takes the form of Kashyapa, a Rishi, and accepts two wives, Kadru and Vinata. Kadru says she wants to be the mother of many children, so she becomes the mother of serpents. Vinata says she wants fewer but stronger children. As a result she becomes the mother of Garuda, a mighty hawk.

Garuda is born into slavery. He learns that, having lost a bet, his mother is forced to serve Kadru. Garuda cannot bear the humiliation of serving the Nagas; he is desperate for a way out. The Nagas say, 'The price of your freedom and your mother's freedom is the pot of Amrita that the Devas jealously guard.'

Garuda rises to the sky, with great ease defeats the Devas, and descends from Swarga, pot of Amrita in his hands. Despite having it in his hands, Garuda does not take a sip of the nectar. This detachment pleases Vishnu. He feels Garuda would make a worthy companion. Vishnu blocks Garuda's descent and says, 'If you serve me as my mount, then I will show you the way to liberate yourself and your mother without making the Nagas immortal.' Garuda is all ears.

Instructed by Vishnu, Garuda demands his liberation and his mother's liberation before he hands over the pot of Amrita to the Nagas. 'So be it,' said the Nagas. 'You are free.'

Garuda then places the pot on grass, as promised. He then advises the Nagas to purify themselves with a bath before drinking the nectar. The Nagas, who had waited patiently for Garuda to return with the nectar, rush to the river. While they are away Garuda invites Indra to swoop down and reclaim the

Poster art showing Vishnu and Lakshmi riding Garuda, the eagle

Vishnu and Lakshmi resting on Ananta Sesha, the serpent

pot. Much pleased, the king of the Devas gives a boon to the hawk, 'Henceforth Nagas will be your food. You will incur no sin when you kill them.'

When the Nagas return, they are furious to see that the pot had disappeared. They shout at Garuda for not securing it. 'I am under no obligation to do so; I am no longer your slave,' snarls Garuda.

The unhappy snakes slither on the grass where the pot of Amrita had been placed. This has a magical effect. Since Amrita had been placed on the grass, the grass acquires the power of regeneration — every time a blade of grass is plucked, it grows back. Likewise, the serpents by rolling on the grass also acquire the power of regeneration. From time to time, they can replace their old skin with new skin and stay youthful forever.

Just as the Devas and the Asuras are eternal enemies, so are the Nagas and Garuda. Garuda and the Devas refer to the forces of the sky: the sun, the moon, the wind, the rain and the fire. Nagas and Asuras refer to the regenerating forces of the earth. The former release Lakshmi from the confines of the earth, but only the latter can give birth to her. Vishnu may side with the Devas but he knows the value of Asuras. That is why both the Garuda and the Naga are sacred to Vishnu.

4

TRIVIKRAMA'S SECRET

Ignorance breeds insecurity and arrogance

Image from 13th century Bengal showing
Vishnu flanked by Lakshmi and Saraswati

Lakshmi is the goddess of wealth while Saraswati is the goddess of learning. Lakshmi is dressed in red and bedecked in gold while Saraswati is dressed in white and bereft of gold. Lakshmi brings prosperity wherever she goes, while Saraswati brings peace. The two are rarely seen together.

Lakshmi is typically drawn towards places where Saraswati resides. That is why prosperity always follows peace. However, when Lakshmi comes, attention shifts from Saraswati to Lakshmi. Enraged, Saraswati leaves. In her absence, Alakshmi comes to give her sister, Lakshmi, company. With Alakshmi comes strife. Strife ends peace. And in the absence of peace, prosperity eventually wanes. Lakshmi leaves and there is nothing left.

This is what repeatedly happens to the Devas. When Lakshmi sits beside Indra, he ignores Saraswati and remains an insecure hedonist, which results in the loss of Lakshmi. Lakshmi returns only when good sense prevails and Indra, adequately chastised, surrenders to Vishnu.

This is also what happens to the Asuras. Deprived of all the treasures that come from the ocean of milk, they pursue ascetic practices and attain Saraswati. They obtain a variety of boons from either Shiva or Brahma that makes them near invincible. They defeat Devas, overrun Amravati and acquire Lakshmi. But with the acquisition of wealth and power, they ignore Saraswati, become arrogant, and the resulting hubris heralds their downfall at the hands of Vishnu.

Devas and Asuras focus on either Saraswati or Lakshmi at any one time. Vishnu, however, focuses on both goddesses at all times. Lakshmi is Vishnu's bhoga-patni, connecting him with the earthly needs of man. Saraswati is Vishnu's moksha-patni,

Poster art of Saraswati, goddess of knowledge

connecting him with the spiritual needs of man. He knows the two of them do not see eye to eye and so he keeps Saraswati hidden in his mouth while he keeps Lakshmi at his feet. Thus he manages to create harmony between them.

IN THE *MAHABHARATA*, SHORTLY AFTER establishing the kingdom of Indra-prastha, the Pandavas gamble it away, just like Indra, and lose rights over it for thirteen years. Following this loss of Lakshmi, the Pandavas are subjected to a humiliating exile in the forest during which they regain Saraswati and understand the role of Lakshmi in their life. When the exile is complete, they ask the Kauravas to return their kingdom but the Kauravas cling to Indra-prastha, go back on their word and refuse to part with it. A war is declared between the Pandavas and the Kauravas, each one claiming rights over Indra-prastha. Both go to Krishna for help. Krishna offers them either himself or his army. Arjuna, representing the Pandavas, chooses Krishna. Duryodhana, representing the Kauravas, chooses Krishna's army. The Pandavas thus choose what Krishna 'is' while the Kauravas choose what Krishna 'has'. In the war, the Kauravas lose everything while Pandavas gain both wisdom and kingdom.

The quest for Saraswati is the journey from Brahma to brahman, from jiva-atma to param-atma, from finite to infinite. This is a journey of 'what I have' to 'what I am'. But in Maya, we equate 'what I have' with 'what I am'. Mine becomes me. The more I have, the greater I feel I am. We construct a self-image of ourselves. This is a delusion. This is the path the Asuras take after they are denied wealth and immortality after the churning of the ocean of milk. Rather than pursuing Saraswati, they

Varaha kills the Asura, Hiranayaksha, to ruthlessly remind the Asura that no one can stake claim over the earth.

Varaha rescues the earth.

Miniature painting of Varaha

The union of Bhu-devi and Varaha creates an Asura called Naraka who is killed by Krishna. This event is celebrated each Diwali. In Goa, effigies of Naraka are immolated during festivities.

Bhu-devi declares Varaha to be her guardian, Bhu-pati.

Cave temple carving from Tamil Nadu showing Varaha with Bhu-devi in his arms

pursue Lakshmi. They delude themselves that the acquisition of Lakshmi will make them immortal and all-powerful. They do not realise that despite having Lakshmi, Devas are insecure and eternally anxious.

And so, an Asura called Hiranayaksha drags Bhu-devi, the earth-goddess, to the bottom of the sea and claims her for himself. He declares himself to be her master. This is a delusion. The earth belongs to no one. To claim ownership of her, or parts of her, stems from ignorance.

The abduction of Bhu-devi by Hiranayaksha alarms the Devas who complain to their father, Brahma. Brahma hears Bhu-devi's wailing. In rage, Brahma's nostrils flare. From one of the flaring nostrils emerges a wild boar with long resplendent tusks. It is Vishnu in the form of Varaha!

Varaha plunges into the sea and challenges the Asura, Hiranayaksha, to a duel. The fight is fierce as Hiranayaksha clings to Bhu-devi, refusing to let her go. But in the end, Varaha gores him to death. Varaha then rises up towards the surface, holding Bhu-devi on his snout. The goddess sings songs praising Vishnu. She declares him Bhu-pati, the lord of earth, her husband. He promises to take care of her. 'If anyone treats you with disrespect, they will answer to me,' says Vishnu.

From that day, Vishnu becomes the guardian of earth, watching over Bhu-devi, stretching himself as the sky above. That is why Vishnu is blue as the day-sky and black as the night-sky.

SOME SAY THAT, AS THEY rose, Bhu-devi accepted Varaha as her consort and named him Bhu-pati, lord of the earth. They made love and so passionate was Vishnu's embrace that

Burning of the effigy of Naraka in Goa during Diwali

North Indian palm leaf painting showing the attack on Naraka's citadel

the earth crumpled, causing mountains and valleys to form. As Vishnu plunged his tusks into the earth, the earth became impregnated with the seeds of all kinds of plants.

From the union of Varaha and Bhu-devi, a child was born. His name was Naraka. Though the son of Vishnu, he was an Asura, and like all Asuras he craved power. He invoked Brahma and asked for immortality. When denied that, he said, 'May I be killed if I attack my mother,' sure that he would never harm the earth. Brahma gave Naraka the boon he sought and sure enough, empowered by the boon, he overran the abode of the Devas and laid claim to Indra's umbrella and Aditi's earrings. Naraka was challenged to a duel by Krishna. Naraka saw that beside Krishna sat his queen, Satyabhama. He did not realise that Krishna and Satyabhama were the mortal incarnations of Vishnu and Bhu-devi, in other words they were his parents. He hurled his weapon at Krishna; it hit Satyabhama. In doing so, Naraka had struck his mother. Instantly, he became vulnerable to the weapons of Krishna and was killed as a result.

Images of Naraka, the Asura, are burned along the Konkan coast during Diwali celebrations. Diwali, the festival of lights, coincides with the autumn harvest. It is the festival that celebrates the arrival of Lakshmi. Here the creator of the Asura and the destroyer are both Vishnu, perhaps alluding to the fact that the farmer who sows the seed is also the one who cuts the crop. The festival once again reminds us that to obtain Lakshmi, the Asura needs to be killed year after year.

Bhu-devi is the tangible form of Lakshmi. Lakshmi has another form called Sri-devi, which indicates intangible wealth. It refers to the glory and fame that everyone craves for. Sri-devi is Sachi who sits besides Indra. Bhu-devi is Pulomi who the Asuras

Calendar art showing Vishnu with two forms of Lakshmi: Sri-devi and Bhu-devi

Mysore painting showing Narasimha emerging from a pillar

abduct. Neither is able to hold on to either. Both Bhu-devi and Sri-devi end up with Vishnu.

NATURE HAS GIVEN ALL LIVING creatures two things to survive, either strength or cunning. In the quest for immortality, Hiranayaksha uses strength. He fails. So his brother, Hiranakashipu takes recourse to cunning. He invokes Brahma and says, 'If you cannot grant me immortality then let me be killed only by a creature that is neither man nor animal, by neither a weapon nor a tool, neither inside a dwelling nor outside, neither on earth nor in the sky, neither at day nor at night.' The boon is given and naturally Hiranakashipu assumes he can never be killed, hence he will never die. 'If I cannot die,' he says, 'I must be spiritual reality. I must be God.'

Here Hiranakashipu uses Saraswati to acquire immortality, hence Lakshmi. Saraswati is thus, for Asuras, only a means, and not the end. When Saraswati is used for acquisition of Lakshmi, she is called Vidya-Lakshmi. Vidya-Lakshmi increases 'what I have' but does not take 'what I am' towards brahman. Jiva-atma remains jiva-atma, trapped in Maya.

Immortality alone is not the attribute of God. Devas have immortality but they are merely gods, not God, because they are eternally unhappy and insecure, unable to attract or withhold Lakshmi. Besides, Devas are located only above the ground. They do not exist below the ground. God or param-atma exists everywhere.

Hiranakashipu's son, Prahalad, refuses to acknowledge his father as God. He prays to Vishnu alone. An angry Hiranakashipu therefore tortures his son. He has him thrown

Kalighat painting showing killing of Hiranakashipu

in water, but Vishnu saves his devotee from drowning. He has him thrown off a cliff, but Vishnu makes his devotee glide down to the ground. Hiranakashipu then orders his sister, Holika, to walk into fire with Prahalad in her arms. Holika has a boon that fire will never harm her, but to the Asura-king's astonishment, when Holika and Prahalad walk into a huge bonfire, Holika is reduced to ashes while Prahalad escapes unscathed, for Vishnu could reverse a boon given by Brahma. This story is told during the festival of Holi when a huge bonfire is lit as winter gives way to spring.

Finally Hiranakashipu asks his son for an explanation. Prahalad says, 'Vishnu is the master of space and time. By tricking death away, you may have conquered time. But you have not conquered space. You are here but only Vishnu is everywhere. That is why Vishnu is God but you are not.'

Hiranakashipu is not convinced. He challenges Prahalad, 'Are you saying this Vishnu is even in the pillars of my palace?' Prahalad nods his head. To prove him wrong, Hiranakashipu kicks and breaks one of the stone pillars of his palace. As the pillar falls apart, to his astonishment a living creature emerges from the stone. It is a strange creature, neither human nor animal. It is Narasimha, half-lion and half-human. Narasimha catches the Asura with his claws, which is neither a weapon nor a tool. He drags the Asura to the threshold of the palace, which is located neither inside a dwelling nor outside. He places the Asura on his thigh, which is neither on earth nor in the sky. At twilight, which is neither day nor night, Narasimha rips open Hiranakashipu's entrails and drinks his blood. Thus the cunning Asura who tried to outsmart death is outsmarted by God.

Having consumed an Asura's blood, Vishnu is said to have

Clay doll from Andhra Pradesh showing Lakshmi seated on Narasimha's thigh

become bloodthirsty. The goddess Lakshmi had to appear and sit on his lap to calm him down. Having calmed down, Narasimha blessed Prahalad.

HIRANAKASHIPU CANNOT IMAGINE THE EXISTENCE of a creature that can be part human and part animal. He cannot imagine an organism that can be born out of a stone pillar. In other words, Vishnu defies his imagination. This episode in Vishnu lore is a reminder that divinity cannot be limited by human imagination or human memory. There is always something in the universe that surprises us.

This is a recurring theme in Vishnu lore. In the *Ramayana*, when Sita sees a golden deer and begs Ram to fetch it for her, Lakshman says that such a creature cannot exist; it is unnatural. To this Ram says, 'Never presume to know the limits of nature. Prakriti is infinite. The human mind is finite.'

In the *Mahabharata*, the warlord Bhishma, commander of the Kaurava army, reveals that he cannot be killed unless he is made to lower a bow and he will lower a bow before no man. In other words, to kill Bhishma one must bring a woman before him. But women are not allowed on the battlefield. This makes it impossible to kill Bhishma and so for nine days the battle on Kurukshetra between the Pandavas and the Kauravas is a stalemate. Finally, Krishna advises the Pandavas to let Shikhandi ride into battle on his chariot with Arjuna and challenge Bhishma to a duel. Shikhandi is born a woman but later in life, with the help of a Yaksha, has acquired male genitals. Thus Shikhandi believes he is a man. But Bhishma does not accept this gender transformation and insists on treating Shikhandi as a

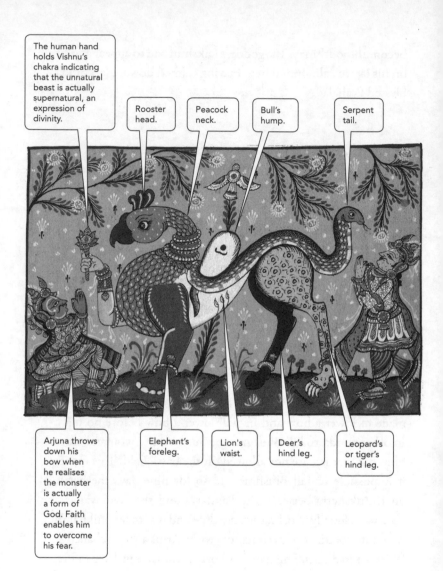

The human hand holds Vishnu's chakra indicating that the unnatural beast is actually supernatural, an expression of divinity.

Rooster head.

Peacock neck.

Bull's hump.

Serpent tail.

Arjuna throws down his bow when he realises the monster is actually a form of God. Faith enables him to overcome his fear.

Elephant's foreleg.

Lion's waist.

Deer's hind leg.

Leopard's or tiger's hind leg.

Patta painting of Nava-gunjara, the composite beast, described in the Oriya *Mahabharata*

woman. Bhishma lowers his bow as Shikhandi rides before him on Krishna's chariot and provides Arjuna with the opportunity to strike him down. Thus the story shows Vishnu accepting gender ambiguity. Bhishma dies because he refuses to make room for ambiguity.

In the Tamil retelling of the *Mahabharata*, one finds the story of a warrior Aravan, son of Arjuna. In order to win the war, the Pandavas are advised to sacrifice a man with sacred marks on his body. There are only three such men in the Pandava camp: Krishna, Arjuna and Aravan. Since Krishna and Arjuna are indispensable, Aravan volunteers to be the sacrifice. But he has one condition, 'I want to marry, experience conjugal bliss before I die. I want to leave behind a widow who will weep for me with true feelings when I die.' So the Pandavas go in search of a bride for Aravan. But no woman is willing to marry a man doomed to die after the wedding night. Finally Krishna decides to take matters into his hands. He takes the form of Mohini and marries Aravan. They spend a night together and at dawn, when Aravan is beheaded, Krishna weeps for him as a widow would.

In the Oriya retelling of the *Mahabharata*, the great archer Arjuna is once confronted by a beast that is a composite of nine animals: it has the head of a rooster; the neck of a peacock; the back of a bull; the waist of a lion; the feet of an elephant, a human, a deer, and a tiger; and a serpent for a tail. At first Arjuna is terrified by this strange beast and raises his bow to shoot it. But then he notices the creature holds in his human hand Krishna's sacred wheel. Arjuna stops. He ponders on his inability to identify the monster or explain its existence. It is clearly beyond all known definitions; it challenges conventional classifications. It seems to emerge from beyond

Image of Vaman from a step-well in Patan, Gujarat

the limits of human comprehension. Arjuna concludes this is no monster but a manifestation of the divine. This is Krishna. This is God. For what is impossible in human reason is possible in divine thought. Arjuna drops his bow and salutes this magical manifestation of God.

HIRANAYAKSHA USES STRENGTH TO OVERCOME his discontent and become all-powerful Hiranakashipu uses cunning. The Asuras who follow, Virochan and Bali, use generosity to win the affection of subjects to achieve the same end. While Hiranayaksha and Hiranakashipu are self-absorbed, Virochan and Bali are concerned about others. This indicates growth. Unlike Hiranayaksha and Hiranakashipu who exclude others, Virochan and Bali include others. Though Asuras, they are revered in the scriptures.

But still, the focus of Virochan and Bali remains 'what I have' rather than 'what I am'. They feel that happiness comes when material needs are met. They fail to realise that as long as man is in Maya, material needs can never be fully satisfied. Contentment comes only when material growth is accompanied by spiritual growth.

Virochan is Prahalad's son. And like all stories of Asuras, he becomes very powerful until Vishnu comes to him in the form of Mohini and secures a gift from him. 'Whatever you wish,' says Virochan. Mohini immediately asks him for his head. Virochan, true to his word, severs his neck, to the delight of the Devas.

Virochan's son, Bali, becomes more powerful than any other Asura before him. And like his father, he is very generous. This makes Bali a very popular Asura. In his realm there is prosperity

Shukra, the guru of Asuras, loses an eye when he tries to stop Bali from giving land to the dwarf.

Bali ritually expresses his commitment to give the dwarf land by giving him water.

Modern sculpture in Kerala, of the giant Trivikrama

everywhere. His fame spreads far and wide and in time eclipses even the glory of the Devas. Humans turn to Bali with reverence and eventually even Sachi leaves Indra's side to sit beside the wise and noble Bali. So great is Bali that in his kingdom everything is perfect; all needs are satisfied and all wants are met; there is no disease or death. People conclude that Bali must be God. Even Bali comes to believe that he is God, after all he can give everyone whatever they desire.

That is when Vishnu approaches Bali as a dwarf or Vaman. 'Whatever you wish shall be yours,' says Bali. Vaman asks for three paces of land. Without a thought, Bali agrees to give what Vaman wants. But Shukra, advisor to Bali, recognises Vishnu. He tells Bali to hold back, but Bali refuses to go back on his word.

To complete the act of charity, Bali has to ritually pour water from the snout of his water pot. To block the ritual, Shukra reduces his size, enters the pot and blocks the snout. Vishnu divines what Shukra is up to and so when no water comes out of the pot, he offers to unclog the snout. Vishnu takes a blade of grass, sharpens its end and shoves it up the snout, blinding Shukra in one eye. Shukra leaps out of the pot howling in pain and water gushes out from the snout. The ritual is thus completed and Vaman is officially entitled to three paces of land.

Vaman then, right before Bali's eyes, transforms into a giant and with one stride claims the sky and with another stride claims the earth. 'I have no other place to place my foot now,' says Vishnu in a voice that booms across the three worlds. Bali, overwhelmed by the sight of the giant Vishnu, bows his head humbly and replies, 'Please place it on my head then.' Vishnu places his head on Bali's head and shoves him under the

Calendar art showing Vishnu as Trivikrama

ground, into Patala, the subterranean world that is the rightful place of Asuras.

All those who see this gigantic form of Vishnu conclude that only Vishnu is Trivikrama, conqueror of the three worlds of the Devas, the Manavas and the Asuras. He spans all worlds. He is God.

Bali is a good king who, like his father, assumes that if he satisfies the desires of all living creatures, all will be well. By transforming into a giant, Vishnu draws Bali's attention to a reality that Bali ignores: human desires are infinite while material resources are finite. Bali can never satisfy *all* the desires of living creatures. Material resources are limited but human want is unlimited. To make Bali realise this, Vaman turns into a giant. Before Vaman's gigantic form, Bali realises his insignificance.

In Vishnu lore, there is a general discomfort with the idea of offering people whatever they desire. A man who offers another 'whatever he or she desires' is in effect being arrogant and over-estimating his capability and capacity. This offer always lands them into trouble.

In the *Ramayana*, Dashratha offers his wife, Kaikeyi, whatever she desires, not once but twice. So she asks that Ram, the heir to the throne, be sent into forest-exile for fourteen years while Bharata, her son, be made king instead. Thus the boon of the king causes trouble and disturbs the serenity of the land.

In the *Mahabharata*, Shantanu offers the same boon to his wife Ganga and she demands that he never question her actions. He agrees only to find to his horror that she drowns their children as soon as they are born. Thus no good comes from these apparently magnanimous boons which in effect are products of delusion for no one, but God, can offer another 'whatever he or she desires'.

Clay doll from Andhra Pradesh — Vishnu with two consorts

Every jiva-atma in the cosmos has boundaries and limits. Devas therefore are restricted to the celestial realms, Manavas are restricted to the earthly realms while Asuras are restricted to the subterranean realms. Asuras, in their quest for fulfilment, constantly seek conquest of realms beyond their own. They rise and occupy other worlds, until Vishnu shows them their place, as in the story of Vaman and Vali.

But each year, Bali is allowed to rise up above the ground. His arrival is marked by many festivals such as Diwali in north India and Onam in Kerala. It is a time of bounty and prosperity. To get the harvest to the granary, Bali has to be killed, like all Asuras. Only when shoved underground, will he return the following year, nourished by Sanjivani Vidya, with yet another bountiful harvest.

ASURAS AND DEVAS ARE QUITE similar to each other. Both are children of Kashyapa, grandchildren of Brahma and hence very aware of their mortality. They both crave Lakshmi, believing that her presence will give them happiness. Both ignore Saraswati and end up losing Lakshmi and with it, happiness.

Asuras and Devas are also very dissimilar. While Devas seek stability, Asuras seek growth. Devas are content with what they have but are insecure about losing it. They do not aspire for more. They do not seek to go beyond the limits of Swarga. Indra never tries to be ruler of the three worlds. But Asuras yearn to be masters of the three worlds. They are never content with what they have. They do not want to be restricted to the subterranean realms. They also want to be masters of the earth and the sky.

Devas and Asuras reflect two aspects of human personality:

Mysore paintings of (clockwise) Varaha, Narasimha and Vamana

our need for stability and our need for growth. The former makes us either insecure or complacent. The latter makes us frustrated and restless. We crave for Lakshmi mostly. Sometimes we crave for Saraswati, with the sole pursuit of obtaining Lakshmi; for when Lakshmi arrives we ignore Saraswati to our peril. That we experience these emotions is an indicator that we have not yet realised or experienced spiritual reality, which is Vishnu.

Vishnu overpowers Hiranayaksha with force and outsmarts Hiranakashipu with cunning. In the case of Vaman, it is Vishnu who transforms and humbles Bali, reminding him that the point of existence is not conquest of the three worlds, but the realisation of infinite potential or brahman. This demands not just material growth but also emotional and intellectual growth, which manifests into generosity of spirit and humility.

VISHNU'S ACTIONS AGAINST HIRANAYAKSHA, HIRANA-KASHIPU and Bali in favour of Indra may seem like God is taking sides. So one can quickly conclude that Asuras are bad and Devas are good. But this is a simplistic explanation. Devas are insecure and complacent, and highly susceptible to overindulgence. This hardly makes them models of appropriate conduct. By contrast, the Asuras, at least Virochan and Bali, are generous and they seem more like wronged heroes rather than villains. And Prahalad, though Asura, is one of the greatest devotees of Vishnu.

The idea of bad gods and good demons is confounding. But it emerges from the presumption that the division of gods and demons is made on ethical and moral terms. This is, more often than not, the result of poor English translations of Hindu

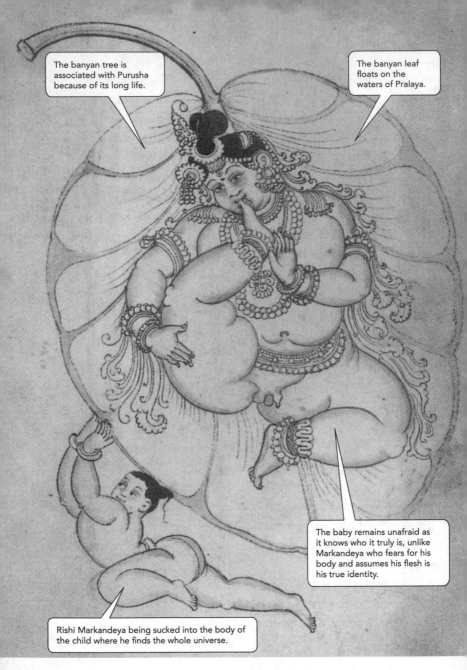

Mysore painting of the child on the banyan leaf

mythology in the 18th century, which declared Devas as 'good' and Asuras as 'bad'.

Devas and Asuras, in mythology, are just two sets of beings, one residing in the sky and the other residing under the earth. Vishnu's actions are driven by the need for social order. He keeps pushing Asuras back where they belong each time they cross their frontiers. The act of killing Asuras generates Lakshmi for the Devas. But while the Devas can enjoy Lakshmi, they are unable to create her. For that they always need the Asuras. Thus Asuras are an essential part of the Hindu universe.

The word evil is often used to describe Asuras. But this word 'evil' makes no sense in Hinduism. Evil means 'the absence of God'. This idea does not exist in Hinduism because, for Hindus, the whole world is a manifestation of the divine. So, nothing can be evil. This notion that everything is divine is made explicit in many stories of Vishnu.

Once when Yashoda sees her little son eating dirt she forces him to open his mouth and is stunned to find in his mouth the earth and all the planets and the stars and everything that makes up the universe. The son is Krishna, Vishnu incarnate.

Once the sage Markandeya has a vision of the world coming to an end. He sees the ocean rise up and consume the earth. Everything is dissolved — the plants, the animals, the rocks and every creature imaginable until there is not a single trace of life. Markandeya weeps for the world there was until he observes a banyan leaf floating on the waves of the ocean. On the leaf is a child; it is Vishnu. The baby inhales and the sage finds himself being sucked into Vishnu's body. Within he sees a magnificent sight: all the oceans and the continents and the stars and the planets. He sees all creatures, those that walk the earth, those

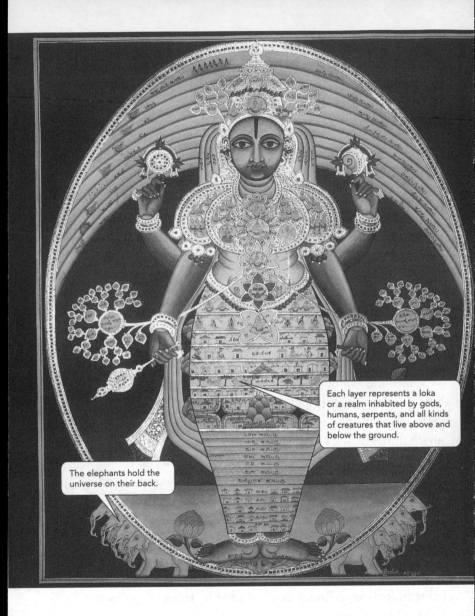

Each layer represents a loka or a realm inhabited by gods, humans, serpents, and all kinds of creatures that live above and below the ground.

The elephants hold the universe on their back.

Tanjore painting of Virat-Swarup

who live in the sky and those who live under the earth. He sees every plant and animal and creature, human and celestial, inside Vishnu. He then is exhaled out of God's body. He realises that all things exists within God.

On the battle field of Kurukshetra, when Krishna gives his discourse known as the *Bhagavad Gita* to Arjuna, Arjuna is convinced that his friend, Krishna, is no ordinary man. 'Show me your true form,' he begs Krishna. And so Krishna shows his Virat-Swarup or cosmic form. He expands till his head reaches beyond the stars and his feet below the deepest recesses of earth. He sprouts innumerable heads and arms and legs. The sun and moon are his eyes. He breathes in worlds and breathes out fire. He grounds planets between his teeth. Within him is time, past and present and future. Within him is space, all dimensions, known and unknown. He is the container of all things.

All things contain the Asuras too. Everything contains the spark of divinity, even those deemed demons and villains by storytellers.

EVIL REFERS TO AN ACT that has no cause or explanation, an act that cannot be justified. But in Hinduism, all actions have a cause. The Hindu world is governed by the notion of karma: no event is spontaneous, everything is a result of past action, either performed in this lifetime or in the ones before.

The idea of evil is typically found in cultures and religions that believe in one life; Hinduism believes in rebirth where deeds of past lives explain everything. Thus in the Hindu world there is no need for the word evil. This idea is made explicit in the story of Jaya and Vijaya.

Poster art of Sanat-kumars, the four boy sages

The behaviour of Hiranayaksha and Hiranakashipu is traced back to their past life, when they were Jaya and Vijaya, doorkeepers of Vaikuntha, the abode of Vishnu.

When the Sanat-kumars seek entry into Vaikuntha, they are stopped at the gates by Jaya and Vijaya as Vishnu is asleep at that time. Annoyed, the four sages cursed the doorkeepers, 'May you be born as Asuras away from Vishnu.' The curse immediately takes effect and the two doorkeepers emerge as Asuras from the womb of Diti.

Jaya and Vijaya, now Hiranayaksha and Hiranakashipu, are eager to return to Vaikuntha and so perform vile deeds that will force Vishnu to descend and liberate them. Hiranayaksha uses his strength to drag the earth below the sea. Hiranakashipu uses cunning instead; he tortures his son, Prahalad, who is a devotee of Vishnu.

The villainy of the two brothers is cited as examples of viparit-bhakti or 'reverse-devotion'; in hating God, one remembers God constantly and thereby earns God's affection.

The cries of Bhu-devi and Prahalad reach Vaikuntha and trouble Vishnu. He descends to rescue both them and his former doorkeepers. Vishnu feels sad that the doorkeepers have been punished for doing their duty; he feels it is his duty to liberate them from the Asura flesh. And so as Varaha and Narasimha he kills the two brothers. Death liberates the brothers. Shedding their Asura forms they return as guardians of Vaikuntha.

When this story is told, the act of violence committed by Varaha and Narasimha transforms from an act of divine retribution to an act of divine love. No more are Asuras seen as villains. There is an explanation for their villainy. While

Jaya and Vijaya, the doorkeepers of Vishnu's paradise known as Vaikuntha

it does not condone their act, it makes one judge them less harshly and with more understanding.

THE NAMES OF BOTH JAYA and Vijaya mean victory. But Jaya means spiritual victory, while Vijaya means material victory. Vijaya is conventional victory, victory over the other, over other's minds, a victory where there are winners and losers. Jaya, on the other hand, is victory over oneself, over one's mind, a victory where there are no losers.

At any moment of life, things either go our way or the other way. In the former situation, when things go our way, we are happy. It is the state of Vijaya, material victory, for we have got what we wanted, often at the expense of others. In the latter situation, when things do not go our way, we are unhappy. But unhappiness propels us to introspect on the nature of material things, and question the reason for our emotions. This introspection and questioning reveals to us the mysteries of the world; we realise the true nature of the world. It is the state of Jaya, spiritual victory, for we have learnt something vital.

In Jaya, Saraswati can walk in our direction. In Vijaya, Lakshmi walks in our direction. But the point of life is to experience the two states together. Lakshmi and Saraswati need to arrive simultaneously, not sequentially. Only when Jaya and Vijaya come together does the gateway to Vaikuntha open up on our lives.

5
RAM'S SECRET
Outgrow the beast to discover the divine

A composite modern painting showing the animal and human forms of Vishnu

Vishnu's stories can be divided into two sets: those who function in a timeless realm and those who function within time. The first set deals mostly with Devas and Asuras. The second set deals with Manavas and Rakshasas.

The battle of Devas and Asuras has more to do with timeless issues revolving around wealth creation, emotional security and intellectual growth. The battle between Manavas and Rakshasas has more to do with appropriate social conduct, ethics and morality that is a function of history and geography.

Devas live in the sky and Asuras live under the earth. Their battle is aligned vertically, between the celestial realms and the nether regions. Manavas and Rakshasas live on earth. Their battle is aligned horizontally between culture and nature, between dharma and adharma.

Words like justice, righteousness and goodness do not adequately explain the term dharma because notions of justice, of what is right and good, change over time and are different in different parts of the world. Dharma is the underlying principle that enables man to realise his divine potential through social behaviour.

To understand the words dharma, and adharma, we have to realise the stark divide between humans and the rest of nature. Only humans have the ability to reject the law of the jungle, both positively and negatively. Positive rejection of the law of the jungle means that we empathise and include others in our quest for security and growth. This is dharma. Negative rejection of the law of the jungle means that we exploit others and include all in our quest for security and growth. This is adharma.

Dharma manifests as rules that seek to provide for, and protect, all creatures. This means actions that help the helpless,

Miniature painting of Ram

where the mighty care for the meek. Adharma is the very opposite; taking advantage of the law of the jungle for the benefit of a few at the cost of the rest. Adharma is about domination, territoriality, hoarding, attachment and power. Dharma is about outgrowing these cravings.

Humans who uphold dharma are called Manavas, after Manu, the first human who rejected the law of the fishes. Humans who uphold adharma are called Rakshasas and are often described as demons. Both Manavas and Rakshasas are grandchildren of Brahma, indicating that they are two different frames of mind. The conflict forms the keystone of the epic, *Ramayana*.

RAMAYANA TELLS THE STORY OF Ram, the only avatar of Vishnu to be worshipped as king. It is the story of a man who upheld the code of civilisation and refused to succumb to animal instincts despite every provocation. To appreciate the *Ramayana* one must first hear the story of Prithu and his father, Vena.

The *Bhagavata Purana* refers to a king called Vena who plundered the earth so much that the earth in disgust ran away in the form of a cow. This naturally resulted in chaos. The plants refused to bear fruit and the seeds did not sprout. There was hunger everywhere. Animals cried, humans wailed. The sages then decided to do something about it. They picked up a blade of grass, chanted magical hymns, turned the grass into a potent missile and used it to kill the greedy king. The Rishis then churned Vena's corpse, removed all that was savage and untamed in it, and created a new king from the distilled, purified positive elements. This king was called Prithu, a form of Vishnu.

Miniature paintings showing Prithu chasing and milking the earth-cow

Prithu went to the earth-cow and requested her to provide milk for his subjects but the cow refused. She was still angry. So Prithu raised his bow and threatened to shoot her down with his arrow. 'If you kill me,' said the earth-cow, 'then all of nature will be destroyed and so will all life.' Prithu then argued that without domesticating the earth, he could not feed humanity. He had no choice but to tame the earth, turn the forests into fields, route the water of rivers with canals. 'Do so then in moderation,' said the earth-cow. So Prithu promised to institute dharma through rules that allow culture to thrive without destroying nature.

This is not easy, it must be remembered. Because human life is validated when there is growth. Animals have no such desire to grow. Growth of human civilisation involves the domestication of nature, the uprooting of forests and destruction of ecosystems. This material growth can destroy the world if unchecked. The only way to check it is by tempering it with intellectual growth and emotional growth, which are the two limbs of spiritual growth.

Dharma balances nature and culture, between the needs of animals and the needs of humans. The symbol of dharma is the bow, which the gods gave to Prithu. The bow indicates balance — the string cannot be left loose or too taut. Prithu is described as the first responsible king of earth. This is why the earth is called Prithvi.

AS HUMAN SOCIETY CREATES SETTLEMENTS, forests are turned into fields and animals are domesticated. This gives man extra resources — more food and time. This enables man to move from material pursuits to other pursuits, such as art and

Kerala mural showing Ram in court

philosophy. But to ensure that there is no excessive material exploitation of earth, rules are put in place. These rules are known as varna-ashrama-dharma.

Varna-dharma means every human being has to function as per his station in life, while ashrama-dharma means every human being has to function as per his stage in life. Thus, in dharma, humanity is governed by duty, not desire. Rules are not ends in themselves; they are warning signs so that greed does not rear its ugly head.

There are four stations in society: Brahmana, the station involved with spiritual activities; Kshatriya, the station involved in administrative activities; Vaishya, the station involved in wealth-generating activities; and Shudra, the station involved in service-providing activities.

Varna means disposition. Jati means profession. In an ideal world, varna corresponds to jati. But this is rarely the case. If it were so, then varna would supersede jati, as varna is natural while jati is man-made. When jati supersedes varna, when professional station is given more importance than natural disposition, problems emerge.

There are four stages, or Ashramas, of life: Brahmacharya, the student stage; Grahastha, the householder stage; the Vanaprastha, the retirement stage; and Sanyasa, the hermit stage. Ashrama ensures that not more than two generations utilised the earth's resources at any one time. When the grandson is born, it is time to retire, eat less food than the householder. And when the great grandson is born, it is time to become a hermit, eat what the forest, not the field, provides.

The role of instituting and maintaining dharma in society is given to the king, who is treated as the diminutive double of

Stone sculpture of Vishnu seated on Garuda

Vishnu.

Like Vishnu seated on a hooded-serpent, he has to stay alert and ensure everybody behaves as expected of their station and stage. If things go wrong, he has to rush as Vishnu would rush on his eagle to set things right. Like Vishnu, he has to blow the conch-shell trumpet to remind people of their obligations to outgrow animal instincts. Like Vishnu, around whose index finger rotates the wheel, he has to review things periodically to ensure things keep moving. Like Vishnu, he has to wield his mace and lotus, punish law-breakers and reward law-abiders.

Only this will ensure peace and prosperity in the kingdom. And if all kings function as Vishnu does, there will be peace and prosperity across the world. The needs of humans will be satisfied without affecting the needs of animals and plants and the regenerative capacity of earth. Only if the king does his duty will the earth cow be happy.

BUT IN THE MATERIAL WORLD nothing is permanent. As faith in spiritual reality collapses, fear resurfaces, duty gives way to desire, ambition rears its ugly head, and eventually rules are compromised. Humans refuse to function as per their station in society and stage of life. The excesses of man breaks the back of the earth-cow and makes her udders sore. In despair, she turns to her guardian, Vishnu. And he responds by descending in various forms, sometimes animal, sometimes human. These descents are known as avataranas and the form Vishnu takes each time is known as avatar.

The number of avatars varies. The most popular list based on Jayadeva's 12th-century song, *Gita Govinda*, has ten:

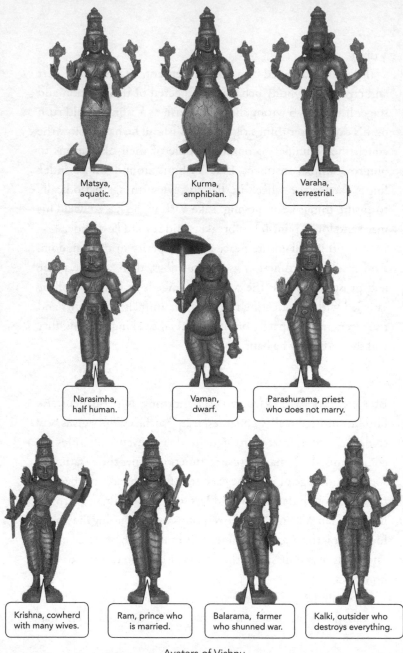

Matsya, aquatic.

Kurma, amphibian.

Varaha, terrestrial.

Narasimha, half human.

Vaman, dwarf.

Parashurama, priest who does not marry.

Krishna, cowherd with many wives.

Ram, prince who is married.

Balarama, farmer who shunned war.

Kalki, outsider who destroys everything.

Avatars of Vishnu

Matsya, Kurma, Varaha, Narasimha, Vaman, Parashuram, Ram, Krishna, Buddha and Kalki. In the *Bhagavata Purana*, there are twenty-two avatars. The other twelve are: Chatursana, Narada, Nara-Narayana, Kapila, Dattatreya, Yagna, Rishabha, Prithu, Dhanvantari, Mohini, Vyasa and Balarama. Others included in the list of avatars are: Hamsa and Hayagriva.

Vishnu's rescue is material — destruction of forces that threaten the natural and social order. The rescue is also spiritual — enlightening creatures so that they do not threaten natural and social order.

It has often been commented that the order of Vishnu's descents follows the evolution of man: the aquatic Matsya, then the amphibian Kurma, then the terrestrial Varaha, followed by the half-human Narasimha and finally the human Vaman.

The human avatars, in turn, follow the varna system: Parashurama is a Brahmana who behaves as a Kshatriya, Ram is a Kshatriya by birth and action, Krishna is a Kshatriya by birth but functions as a Vaishya (cowherd) and Shudra (charioteer). They also follow the ashrama-system: Parashurama is a Brahmachari, Ram and Krishna are Grihastis, Buddha becomes a Vanaprasthi and finally, Sanyasi.

WHILE MATERIAL REALITY IS BOUND to transform, Vishnu makes the transformations predictable by anticipating the changes and acting accordingly.

Thus, over time, all organisations and systems and processes and codes lose their relevance. This inevitable and gradual collapse of all systems is expressed in the concept of yuga.

Just as a human life has four phases: childhood, youth,

Clay doll of Vishnu reclining on the serpent with Lakshmi at his feet

maturity and old age, every organisation or system goes through four phases: Krita, Treta, Dvapara and Kali. It is said that the bull of dharma stands on four legs in the Krita yuga, on three legs in Treta yuga, two in Dvapara yuga and one in Kali yuga. After this, the bull of dharma and the society it upholds is washed away by the waters of Pralaya. This is death of the world, followed by rebirth. In the new life, the four yugas will follow each other once again. This is the kala-chakra, or the circle of time.

In the *Bhagavad Gita*, Krishna says, 'Whenever dharma is threatened, I descend to set things right.' This line has to be read with an understanding of yuga. Vishnu does not stop the march of time, nor does he reverse it. An avatar does not restore the ideal dharma, because there is no ideal dharma. An avatar re-defines dharma for a particular age. Dharma of Krita yuga is not the dharma of Treta yuga; times are different, needs are different, hence the code of civilisation is different. One can look at Vishnu as a doctor who appears whenever there is a disease. He restores health but does not stop aging. Eventually, a patient will die. The doctor's duty is to help the patient live a full and healthy life. This is what avatars do: balance human demands with nature's needs for as long as possible. Pralaya is an eventuality, but an avatar prevents it from happening prematurely.

One can say that when one age has reached its ebb, an avatar appears to facilitate the transition to the next age. Parashurama thus appears when the golden age of Krita yuga gives way to the silver age of Treta yuga. Ram appears when the Treta yuga gives way to the bronze age of Dvapara yuga. Krishna appears when the Dvapara yuga gives way to the iron age of Kali yuga. Buddha shows the way in Kali yuga and when Kali yuga comes to a close, Kalki heralds Pralaya — death that leads to rebirth.

Mysore painting of three incarnations of Vishnu, all known as Ram

THE SHIFT FROM KRITA YUGA into Treta yuga happens when the notion of property emerges. Property relates to several things: domesticated animals, land, and even women.

The wife is visualised as property. She is expected to be obedient and faithful to her husband. In the Krita yuga, this is voluntary. But as the golden age draws to a close, desire and passion changes all this. Fidelity is enforced.

Renuka, a princess, marries Jamadagni, a priest. And she bears him five sons, the youngest of whom is Parashurama. Renuka is a faithful wife, so faithful that she can collect water in unbaked pots made of clay from the riverbank. But one day, Renuka sees a handsome Gandharva bathing in the river and sporting with his wives. Some say, it is not a Gandharva but a king called Kartavirya. She is smitten with passion for the handsome man. This momentary adulterous thought causes her to lose her magical powers; she can no longer collect water in unbaked clay pots. When her husband realises this, he is furious. He orders his sons to behead their mother. The elder four refuse and so die instantly. Parashurama, however, picks up the axe and severs his mother's neck. Pleased with this unconditional obedience, Jamadagni offers Parashurama a boon. 'Resurrect my mother back to life,' says Parashurama. Jamadagni does so, for he is a priest of the Bhrigu clan, and like Bhrigu and Bhrigu's son, Shukra, who serve the Asuras, he possesses Sanjivani Vidya, the secret lore of bringing the dead back to life.

In Krita yuga, cows are distributed freely by kings. The act of Kshatriya generosity ensures Brahmanas can carry out their rituals and other spiritual and philosophical obligations without worrying about income. But then Krita yuga draws to a close and Kartavirya, king of the Haihaiya clan, seeks the

Mysore painting of Parashurama

Mysore painting showing Parashurama beheading his mother, Renuka

Miniature painting from north India showing Parashurama killing Kartavirya, the Haihaiya king

return of a cow gifted to Jamadagni. Jamadagni finds the very idea preposterous. No one takes back gifts once given. But the king insists and begins to take the cow by force. Kartavirya is a powerful king, blessed with a thousand arms, a metaphor for his military might, and no one can stop him. Jamadagni begs the king to stop but the king refuses. Parashurama cannot bear to see his father demean himself so. He cannot bear to hear the piteous cries of the cow being dragged away by the king. So he picks up his axe and hacks the king to death. This is a shocking event — the killing of a king by a priest. When the sons of Kartavirya hear of this, they avenge their father's death by raiding Jamadagni's hermitage and cutting his head off. An infuriated Parashurama, takes an oath. To rid the earth of all warriors and kings. So a massacre begins. He kills twenty-one generations, some say twenty-one clans, of Kshatriyas. So much blood flows that it forms five lakes. Parashurama uses the blood of fallen kings to make funeral offerings to his father. He then swears to keep a watchful eye over the kings of the earth who abuse their military might to gain power.

But then one day Parashurama encounters Ram; he realises his work is done, for Ram is the model king, one who never uses his royal power for personal gain. Ram, like Parashurama, is an avatar of Vishnu, but the only one to be visualised and worshipped as a king.

PARASHURAMA, THOUGH BORN IN A family of priests, behaves as a warrior, thus transgressing the rules of varna. Ram, however, is born in a family of kings and all his life behaves in keeping with what is expected of royalty.

Ram and Bharata, brothers who are willing to give their property to each other, transcending animal territorial instincts.

Princes of Ayodhya visualised as humans.

Miniature painting showing brothers

Vali and Sugriva, brothers who fight over property displaying animal territorial behaviour.

Princes of Kishkinda visualised as monkeys.

Chitrakathi painting from Maharashtra showing brothers

He is the eldest son of Dashratha, king of Ayodhya, born of the first wife, and rightful heir to the throne. But on the eve of his coronation, his step-mother, Kaikeyi, reminds Dashratha of a promise made long ago, that he would give satisfy any two of her wishes. She demands that Ram go into exile and live as a hermit in the forest for fourteen years, and her son, Bharata, be made king instead. When informed of the situation, Ram, without regret or resentment, abandons his royal robes and goes to the forest followed by his dutiful wife, Sita and his loving brother, Lakshman. To Kaikeyi's despair, Bharata refuses to take the throne acquired through deceit. He decides to live like a hermit himself and wait for his brother to return and reclaim his right to the throne.

The behaviour of Ram's brothers are very unlike the behaviour of other brothers Ram encounters as he moves from north to south during his exile. Far to the south is the kingdom of Lanka, ruled by Ravana, the Rakshasa who has usurped the throne from his brother, Kubera, the Yaksha. In between Ayodhya and Lanka is Kishkinda, land of monkeys, ruled by Vali, who was supposed to share his kingdom with his brother Sugriva, but following a misunderstanding, kicks him out.

This is not a geographical reference, rather a metaphorical indicator. In mythic vocabulary, north, the realm of the still Pole Star, is indicative of spiritual reality and south, the opposite, is indicative of material reality. And so, the farther one goes from Ayodhya to the south, the *Ramayana* reveals a gradual decay in the principles of dharma and the rise of man's animal and demonic nature.

Chitrakathi painting from Maharashtra of Surpanakha

A calendar print of Ravana abducting Sita

DHARMA IS ABOUT PROPERTY RIGHTS as well as marriage rights. Ram and Sita are described as a couple who are eternally faithful to each other. Ram does not look at another woman, and Sita does not look at another man. They are the ideal couple. Their commitment to each other is repeatedly threatened by the world around.

When a Rakshasa woman, Surpanakha, seeks sexual gratification from Ram, he refuses on grounds that he is already married. The encounter turns ugly as Surpanakha, in keeping with her preference for the law of the jungle, tries to harm Sita. An enraged Lakshman cuts off Surpanakha's nose. Scorned thus, rather than tamed, Surpanakha complains to her brother, Ravana, who in outrage abducts Sita and carries her to his island-kingdom of Lanka, intent on making her one of his many wives. Sita, however, refuses to even look at Ravana. For her, there is no man but Ram.

In the forest, civilisation is gradually abandoned and rules are forgotten. Through force, a man can take his brother's property. Through force, men and women can disregard the marital rights of others. Neither Sita nor Ram let the forest erode their values. Wherever they go, they hold on to the principles of dharma. They may have left Ayodhya, but Ayodhya never leaves them.

IN THE FOREST, RAM ENCOUNTERS a monkey called Sugriva and helps him become king. In exchange, Sugriva offers to help Ram find Sita. Sugriva is bound by his word to help Ram. No such obligation binds another monkey called Hanuman. Hanuman serves Ram anyway. This spirit of generosity indicates spiritual awareness, a concern beyond the self for the other.

Calendar print of Hanuman building the bridge to Lanka

Calendar print of Hanuman revealing Ram in his heart

Hanuman thus breaks free from Prakriti and becomes Purusha.

Animals are governed by their sexual and violent instincts. Humans can overpower these instincts because of their larger brain. Though animal, without the benefit of a larger brain, Hanuman practices celibacy and fights only for the benefit of others. This transforms him into an object of veneration. Though beast, he comes to be equated with God.

Under the leadership of Hanuman, the monkeys build a bridge across the sea to the island-kingdom of Lanka and launch an attack on Ravana's citadel. A king is supposed to be the provider and protector of his people. Ravan is neither; he is the archetypal alpha male for whom kingdom is nothing but territory. He is unwilling to give up Sita even if it means the destruction of Lanka. He sends his brothers and sons to their deaths, but refuses to part with Sita. He wants his way at all cost.

Ravana has ten heads and twenty hands. He is described as the son of a priest, well versed in the scriptures. He is also described as a devotee of Shiva. Despite all this knowledge, and all the powers bestowed upon him, he does not display wisdom. While the monkeys have transformed themselves into humans, Ravana descends from being human to animal. In fact, he is worse than animal, for his actions are not motivated by self-preservation or self-propagation. He is consumed by self-delusion and self-importance and that is ultimately his downfall.

AFTER KILLING RAVANA, RAM RETURNS to Ayodhya with his wife Sita and is crowned king. This marks the dawn of Ram-rajya, the rule of Ram, considered the golden age when dharma is perfectly upheld.

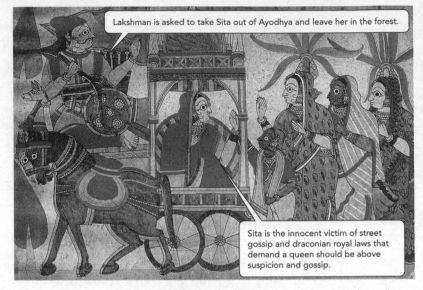

Chitrakathi painting from Maharashtra showing Sita being taken out of Ayodhya

Calendar art showing Sita's twin sons, Luv and Kush

But then, one day, Ram hears street gossip. The people of Ayodhya are embarrassed to have Sita as their queen, for having spent several months as Ravana's captive she is a woman of tainted reputation. Ram promptly abandons Sita and has her sent to the forest, this despite the fact that she proves her fidelity by walking through fire unscathed. This is the controversial conclusion of the *Ramayana*. The obvious injustice is clearly at odds with the principles of dharma.

This episode draws attention to the complexity of dharma. Is Ram the king of Ayodhya first or the husband of Sita? As king, he is obliged to respect the wishes of the people of Ayodhya and the rules of his dynasty, that a woman of tainted reputation cannot be queen. But as husband, he is obliged to protect his wife. Ram chooses to be king first, sacrificing personal joy so that the integrity of the ruling family is never compromised.

One can argue that, as king, he should protect Sita who is, besides being wife and queen, also his subject. But one must remember that as king, Ram is expected not to make rules but to uphold them. This rule is the rule of his clan and he is obligated to uphold it. And Ram submits to it. This tale thus draws attention to the limitations of rules and traditions. The rules and traditions of the Raghu clan, which made Ram obey his father at the start of the epic, turn out to be draconian at the end of the epic when innocent Sita is rejected on grounds of tainted reputation.

But while Ram abandons Sita, the queen, he does not abandon Sita, the wife. He refuses to remarry. Instead he places beside him on his throne the golden effigy of Sita, a reminder that none can take her place. That the metal used to make Sita's image is gold, the purest of metals, is a symbolic representation

Kalamkari cloth painting of Ram;
it is unusual as it shows Ram with a moustache

of what Ram thinks of her character.

Every act in Hindu mythology has a consequence. And the abandonment of Sita has its consequence. After Sita is abandoned, Ram loses the only battle of his life. His royal horse is captured by Luv and Kush, Sita's children, born in the forest, who don't know that Ram is their father. They successfully fend off Ram's army, an indicator that dharma rests with Sita, not with Ayodhya.

Sita stops the war between Ram and his sons. Her victory is clear proof of her purity and chastity. The people of Ayodhya beg her forgiveness and ask her to return to the palace after reaffirming her chastity once more. So Sita asks the earth to open up and swallow her if she has been a faithful wife. The earth immediately opens up and Sita descends to the nether regions. It is in effect the return of Lakshmi to the land of her fathers.

Ram, as Vishnu, refuses to stay on earth without Lakshmi and so, after bequeathing his kingdom to his sons, walks into the river Sarayu and gives up his mortal body.

The final chapter of the *Ramayana* draws attention to the difference between dharma and niti and riti. Niti means law and riti means tradition. Laws and traditions are created in full earnestness to help the helpless. Sometimes they can end up being unfair and cruel. Sita's abandonment is a case in point. When law and tradition fail to uphold the principle of dharma, they need to be abandoned or changed. This thought is elaborated in the story of Krishna.

6

KRISHNA'S SECRET

Know the thought behind the action

Tanjore-style print showing the Krishna of *Bhagavata*

The story of Krishna is spread across two epics: the *Bhagavata* and the *Mahabharata*.

Bhagavata refers to Krishna as the flute-playing, playful, lovable, mischievous, romantic cowherd who loves butter. *Mahabharata* refers to Krishna as the conch-blowing city-builder, warrior, leader, philosopher, statesman and charioteer covered with the grime of war. Together these two Krishnas create the purna-avatar, the most wholesome manifestation of God.

But Krishna is an unusual God. He challenges all conventional notions of divinity and appropriate social conduct. His name literally translates as 'black', challenging the traditional Indian discomfort with the dark complexion. He is visualised as either cowherd or charioteer, never as priest or king, a deliberate association with the lower strata of society. His mother is not his real mother, his beloved is not his wife, and the women he rescues are neither his subjects nor members of his family. His lovemaking is not really lovemaking; his war is not really war. There is always more than meets the eye. And so, only Krishna, of all the avatars, sports a smile, a mischievous, meaningful smile. There is always more than meets the eye, when Krishna is around.

WHILE RAM IS CALLED MARYADA Purushottam, he who upholds rules of society at any cost, Krishna is called Leela Purushottam, he who enjoys the game of life. Unlike Ram, who is serious and serene and evokes respect, Krishna is adorable and rakish, and evokes affection. Ram's story takes place in the second quarter of the world, the Treta yuga, when the bull of dharma stands on three legs. Krishna's story takes place in a later,

A print of Parthasarathy of Chennai

third quarter of the world, the Dvapara yuga, when the bull of dharma stands on two legs. Krishna's world is thus closer to the world we live in, the final quarter or Kali yuga, and shares the hazy morality and ethics we encounter today. In this world, the concept of dharma becomes even more difficult to express and institute. And this is most evident in the story of Yayati.

Yayati, an ancestor of Krishna, is cursed by his father-in-law to become old and impotent when he is discovered having a mistress. Yayati begs his sons to suffer the curse on his behalf so that he can retain his youth. Yadu, the eldest son, refuses to do so because he feels his father should respect the march of time and not feed on the youth of his children. Puru, the youngest son, however, agrees to accept his father's old age. Puru's sacrifice makes Yayati so happy that, years later, when he has had his fill of youth, he declares that the younger Puru will be his heir and not the elder Yadu. Further, he curses Yadu that none of his children or his children's children will be entitled to wear the crown.

Krishna, being Yadu's descendent, is therefore never king. Kingship passes on to Puru's descendents, the Pandavas and Kauravas, even though time and again they demonstrate their unworthiness to wear the crown.

What seems a good thing in Ram's yuga becomes a bad thing in Krishna's yuga. Ram's unquestioning obedience of his father transforms him into God. But Puru's unquestioning obedience results in the collapse of society. Dashratha requests Ram's obedience so that he can uphold his word. Yayati, however, demands the obedience of his children for his own pleasure. Yayati exploits the rule for his own benefit whereas Dashratha enforces the rule so that royal integrity is never questioned.

Devaki never nursed Krishna nor fed him butter, suggesting that this image is that of Yashoda; or the images of the two mothers are blurred; or in this image is fulfilled Devaki's desire to nurse Krishna.

The mother-child image alludes to Mother Mary and Jesus and according to local legend is the reason why this temple was not desecrated by the Portuguese rulers of Goa.

Krishna holds butter in his hand.

Print of Devaki Krishna enshrined at Marcela, Goa

The rule (obey the father) evokes dharma in Dashratha's case, but not so in Yayati's.

Yayati's conduct results in a society where the letter of the law becomes more important than the spirit of the law. This is the world of Krishna, a world where what matters more than the deed is the thought behind the deed.

THE STORY OF KRISHNA BEGINS in Mathura, the city of the Yadavas. It is foretold that the eighth child of Devaki will kill her elder brother, Kamsa. Consumed by fear, Kamsa kills all of Devaki's children as soon as they are born.

The night Devaki delivers her eighth son, her husband Vasudeva takes him across the river Yamuna to Gokul. There, he exchanges his son for the daughter of Yashoda and cowherd-chief Nanda, who is born the same night. Yashoda wakes up to find Krishna in her arms. She assumes this is her son and raises him as a cowherd. Kamsa, meanwhile, tries to kill the girl he finds in Devaki's arms but the child slips out of his grasp, rises into the air, transforms into a goddess and informs him that his killer is safe. Kamsa fumes in frustration as he realises all his attempts to change his destiny have come to naught.

Krishna, as a consequence of his father's actions, ends up with two mothers: Devaki who gives birth to him and Yashoda who raises him. Devaki is a woman of noble rank. Yashoda is a common milkmaid. Devaki represents all the qualities one is born with. Yashoda represents all the qualities one acquires in life. Thus Krishna's divinity, rooted in Devaki's blood and Yashoda's milk, acknowledges both nature and nurture.

We are all a combination of what we are born with as well

Butter is a symbol of love.

Mysore painting showing Krishna stealing butter

Clothes are the symbols of the masks we wear in society.

Nakedness indicates the truth of ourselves that we hide from the world as we adorn our bodies with clothes.

A south Indian temple wall carving showing Krishna stealing clothes

as what we are raised to be. Our natural disposition is known as varna while the cultural indoctrination is jati. Krishna is by varna a nobleman but by jati a cowherd. Though nobleman, he can never be king. Though cowherd, he can always lead.

Our behaviour towards others is based on what we see and how we process our observation. But not all things can be seen. Jati can be seen but not varna. One can see behaviour but one has no access to beliefs. A man can dress as a cowherd and talk like a cowherd, but he may at heart be a prince. We will never know unless we open our eyes to this possibility.

IN KRISHNA'S NARRATIVES, BUTTER, CHURNED out of milk, is the symbol of love. The milkmaids of his village hoard the butter in pots hung high from ceilings, out of everyone's reach. They are only for sale. Krishna protests and demands its free distribution. And so, with a naughty glint in his eye, he climbs on the shoulders of his friends, reaches up to the pots and breaks them with glee, letting the butter of love flow out.

As Krishna grows up, the metaphor of love changes. Pots are no longer broken. Instead clothes are stolen. An embarrassing situation for the gopis bathing in the Yamuna and everyone hearing the story until we realise that in the language of symbols, clothes represent our public face. Krishna notices the sensitive hearts hiding behind each and every public face. This heart is sensitive, yearning to give affection and receive it.

Hearts resist and tongues complain, 'Don't steal our butter, Krishna. Don't steal our clothes, Krishna.' No one wants to be free with love. No one wants to expose the vulnerable heart.

Miniature painting showing the Maha-raas

Everyone marches into Yashoda's house, demanding that Krishna be restrained.

Yashoda tries to stop Krishna but fails. She binds him to a drum, locks him inside the house, but Krishna remains the relentless makkhan-chor and chitt-chor, he-who-steals-butter and he-who-steals-hearts. Until all defences break down, until there are no pots, no clothes, no stinginess with affection, only an open invitation to a heart full of buttery love.

WHEN THE HEART IS OPENED up, when love flows into it and from it, a sense of security prevails. With security comes freedom. There is no need to pretend. We can be ourselves. There is no desire to force our wills on anyone. We accept and embrace everyone, we include people, we allow them to be themselves, because we are accepted and embraced by God. The result is Maha-raas in the flowery meadow on the banks of the Yamuna, known as Madhuvan.

The Maha-raas, where Krishna plays the flute surrounded by a circle of dancing milkmaids, is a symbolic representation of absolute spontaneity. No formal relationship dictates Krishna's affection for the milkmaids. Unfettered by social restriction, it is created by emotions that are simple, innocent, with no underlying motive. That is why it takes the form of a circle, the most spontaneous of natural shapes. Between God in the centre and his devotees in the circumference only a radius of mutual unconditional affection prevails.

So long as the milkmaids love Krishna unconditionally without fetters, he multiplies himself and dances with each one of them, making each one feel completely and fully loved.

Kerala painting of
Krishna taming the heron

Mysore painting of
Krishna killing Putana

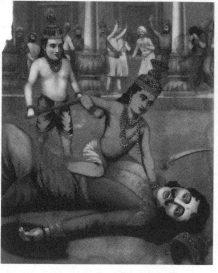

Orissa painting of Krishna subduing
the serpent Kaliya in the river

Calendar art showing Krishna
overpowering Kamsa

But when they become possessive and refuse to share him with others, Krishna disappears and fills the women with despair. When realisation dawns and they beg forgiveness, Krishna returns to Madhuvan to dance the dance of love.

The Maha-raas takes place outside the village, in the forest, at night, away from familiar surroundings. Yet the women feel safe. They are unthreatened by the law of the jungle. They have faith in Krishna and no fear. When Krishna plays the flute in the middle of the jungle, love — not force — prevails. The weakest, the most unfit, are not afraid. They can sing, dance and thrive in joyous abandon.

BUT KRISHNA'S ABODE IS NOT the jungle. First he lives in the village of Gokul, and later his parents migrate to Vrindavan, as Gokul becomes increasingly unsafe. These villages are domesticated spaces. Domestication of the land involves violence, the forcible removal or suppression of wild forces that threaten the settlement.

Krishna is threatened several times in his childhood. He is threatened by a wet-nurse, Putana, who carries poison in her breasts. He is threatened by natural forces: a whirlwind, a forest fire and torrential rain. He is threatened by animals: a wild horse, an errant calf, a ferocious bull, a python, a crane and a donkey. He is even threatened by cartwheels rolling down the street. As Krishna defends himself and protects his village from these various threats, he becomes violent. The demons are killed or driven away. The wild beasts are subdued and their spirit is broken as they are tamed. The forest fire is swallowed and a mountain raised to protect the village from the wet torrential downpour.

Devotees continue to treat Ranchhod Krishna as the cowherd Krishna even though there are no cows or milkmaids in the shrine.

The temple of one who withdrew from the battlefield is ironically located in land associated with Rajputs and other warrior communities who preferred death to withdrawal.

Krishna bears symbols of Vishnu such as conch-shell and wheel.

A print of Ranchhodji Krishna enshrined in Dwarka

Thus Krishna acknowledges the violence that is implicit in human survival. More than the act of violence, what matters is the thought behind the violence. The demons seek to hurt Krishna because his existence threatens Kamsa; their violence is rooted in Kamsa's fear and his refusal to accept his fate. Such violence is adharma. Krishna's violence is defensive, rooted in the human need to survive and thrive; he does not want to hurt or exploit anyone. His violence is therefore dharma.

WHEN KAMSA HEARS OF THIS remarkable cowherd in Vrindavan who kills demons and tames wild beasts and holds mountains up with his little finger, he is convinced that this is his long lost nephew, his nemesis. Determined to change his fate and intent on killing him, he invites Krishna to a wrestling match in his city of Mathura, and sends a royal chariot to fetch him.

But things do not go as planned. The charismatic lad not only overpowers the mighty wrestlers of Mathura, he also kills the royal elephant, breaks the royal bow and finally attacks and kills the wicked king, to the delight of all the Yadavas who have grown tired of Kamsa's excesses.

The killing of Kamsa is unique because it is the only story in Hindu mythology where a father-figure is killed. Unlike Ram who submits to Dashratha, and Yadu who submits to Yayati, Krishna refuses to submit to Kamsa. This tale marks a shift in thinking where the younger generation refuses to suffer the tyranny of the older generation. This makes Krishna a radical hero in the Hindu spiritual landscape.

When the royal chariot carrying Krishna rolled out of Vrindavan for Mathura, the milkmaids had feared that Krishna

Kerala mural of Krishna getting married

Mysore painting of Krishna with many wives

would never return. Krishna had assured them that he would, as soon as the wrestling match was over. But after the killing of Kamsa, Krishna's true identity is revealed. He is Devaki's son, not Yashoda's. He is a Yadava nobleman, not a common cowherd. Destiny has other plans for him and he must submit to it. He cannot return to the land of milk and butter and cows and milkmaids, the land of his pleasure. His tryst with kings has begun.

Kamsa's father-in-law, Jarasandha, attacks the city of Mathura to avenge Kamsa's death and burns it to the ground. Rather than fight to the death, Krishna withdraws from the battlefield and takes the Yadavas westwards to the safety of the island-city of Dwarka, far from Jarasandha's influence. This display of discretion over valour is uncharacteristic of warriors and once again positions Krishna as an unconventional hero, one who accepts the inglorious epithet of Ran-chor-rai, the warrior who withdrew from battle. Krishna lives to fight another day.

AMONGST ALL THE MILKMAIDS OF Vrindavan, there is one who is identified as being closest to Krishna. Her name is Radha. Radha is said to be the wife of Yashoda's brother and she is older than Krishna. Theirs thus is a relationship that transcends custom and law. In their pure love, unbound by expectations, unanchored by conventions, there is music. It inspires Krishna to play the flute.

But when Krishna leaves Vrindavan, he enters a world of customs and laws, where no relationship is pure, where everything is fettered by expectations. The music stops. He gives up his flute and instead takes up the conch-shell of warriors. He goes about

Calendar art showing the five Pandavas and their common wife, Draupadi

marrying women — not for love, but out of a sense of duty.

He elopes with and marries Rukmini, princess of Vidarbha, after she begs him to save her from a loveless marriage she is being forced into. He marries Satyabhama, who is given to him as a token of gratitude, when he identifies the killer of her uncle and recovers a very precious jewel, the Syamantaka, belonging to her family. He ends up with eight principal wives and later gets 16,100 junior wives, women who seek refuge with him after he kills Naraka, the demon-king who held them captive in his harem.

Krishna is a good husband to all these women and a good father to their children. He multiplies himself several fold so that he can give each wife individual attention and no wife feels abandoned or excluded. But none of the wives sees the passion in his eyes that is reserved for Radha, nor do they dance around him as the milkmaids did in the forest. The relationship here is much like Ram's relationship with Sita, formal, dictated by custom, based on respect not passion.

Krishna does not receive love from his maternal uncle, Kamsa. But he ensures the same is not the fate of the Pandavas, his cousins. Their maternal uncle is Krishna's father, Vasudev.

Krishna finds his aunt, Kunti, and her sons in abject poverty, having been denied their inheritance by their father's brother, the blind Dhritarasthra and his hundred sons, the Kauravas. The only thing the five Pandavas have going for them is that they share a common wife, Draupadi, princess of Panchala, who is no ordinary woman, but Lakshmi.

When Vishnu is Parashurama, Lakshmi takes the form of his father's cow. In other words, she is his mother, providing him

Modern painting showing Krishna replacing Draupadi's clothes
as the Kauravas try to disrobe her

nutrition. When Vishnu is Ram, Lakshmi takes the form of Sita, his faithful wife, who stands by his side at all times. When Vishnu is Krishna, Lakshmi takes the form of Draupadi, not his mother or his wife, but a distant relative, barely connected by blood or marriage. Draupadi cares for Krishna as Radha does, without expectations. And that is why Krishna always watches over her, even though he is not obliged to.

With Draupadi as their wife and Krishna as their friend, the Pandavas demand from their uncle their half of the family inheritance. After much deliberation, they are given the forest of Khandavaprastha. With the help of Krishna, they transform this forest into the prosperous kingdom of Indraprastha.

With Krishna behind them, the Pandavas turn into a lethal force. Bhima, the mightiest Pandava, kills Jarasandha, destroyer of Mathura, in a duel. And Yudhishtira, the eldest Pandava, earns the right to declare himself a sovereign king.

Unfortunately, success goes to the head of the Pandavas. And while Krishna is away, they accept an invitation from the Kauravas to a gambling match. There they gamble away everything — not just gold and cows, but also their newfound kingdom, their own liberty and even their wife.

This gambling match is an indicator of the collapse of dharma for it shows kings treating culture as property. They have forgotten why dharma was instituted and kingdoms established in the first place: to create extra material resources so that man can look beyond survival and look for meaning.

That Krishna is not by their side when the Pandavas are gambling away everything indicates the lack of spiritual awareness. They become like Devas who lose Lakshmi.

Having managed to wrench away from the Pandavas every-

Mughal miniature showing Krishna negotiating peace with the Kauravas

thing they possess, the Kauravas, like Asuras, are consumed by megalomania. Instead of protecting the helpless, as kings are supposed to, they exploit the situation, like Rakshasas.

Draupadi, gambled away by her five husbands, now a Kaurava slave, is dragged by her hair, brought to the gambling hall and disrobed in public. She demands justice, appeals to clemency, but no one comes to her rescue. Everyone hides behind the letter of the law. The spirit of dharma is totally forgotten as Draupadi screams in horror and raises her arms in utter helplessness.

This is when Krishna reveals his divinity. Miraculously, bending space and time, Krishna ensures that every cloth that is removed from Draupadi's body is replaced by another cloth. This is Vishnu acting as Govinda, the cowherd, protecting the earth-cow who is being abused by her so-called guardians, the kings. He promises to rid the earth of such unrighteous kings. He promises to wash her tears with their blood.

A PACT IS REACHED. THE Pandavas and their wife will live in forest exile for twelve years followed by a year incognito. If in the final year they escape identification then the Kauravas promise to restore to the Pandavas all that they gambled away.

'Why can we not fight and take back what is ours right away? Why should we suffer thirteen years of humiliating exile?' demand the Pandavas. To this Krishna says, 'Because you have given your word. And because only this way will you be cleansed of the crime of gambling your kingdom away.'

For thirteen years, the Pandavas suffer the exile. During this time, their children live with Krishna. It is during such times of crisis that Saraswati returns to the Pandavas. Each brother

Modern painting showing Arjuna before the war

Mysore painting showing Arjuna during the war

admits their flaws and faults and emerges a stronger man. They meet sages and learn what the point of kingship is, what the point of material security is and the reason one must aspire for spiritual growth. It is during the exile, especially the final year spent living as servants in the court of King Virata, that the Pandavas make themselves worthy of kingship.

After thirteen years of exile, the Pandavas emerge cleansed but the Kauravas remain corrupt as ever, refusing to keep their word, refusing to even compromise, Krishna says, 'For the sake of peace at least give your cousins five villages.' But Duryodhana, the eldest of the Kauravas, refuses to part with even a needlepoint of land. It is then that Krishna encourages the Pandavas to declare war on the Kauravas.

This war is not for property. This war is about dharma. And dharma is about outgrowing the animal instinct of territoriality and discovering the human ability to share and care. The Kauravas refuse to share their wealth with their own brothers. They refuse to keep their word and use force to usurp other people's wealth. The earth cannot be burdened by such kings. They have to be killed.

LIKE THE MAHA-RAAS, THE WAR at Kurukshetra is not what it seems. Both are paradoxes. The sexuality of the former is not about sex and the violence of the latter is not about violence. Beneath the unabashed clandestine sexuality of the Maha-raas is the absence of desire for any physical conquest; it is about perfect love and absolute security that allows married women to dance and sing all night in the forest with a divinely handsome boy. Likewise, the

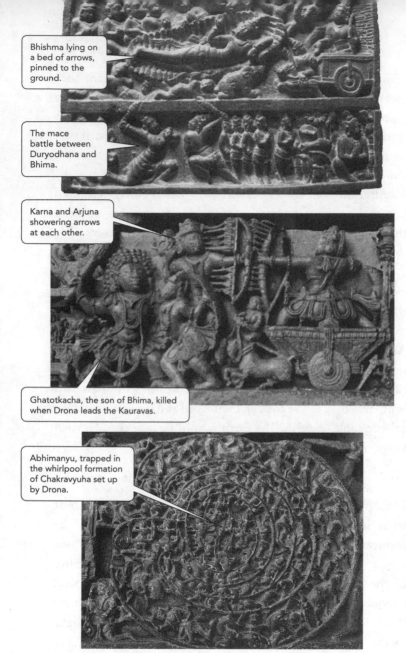

Temple wall carvings from Pattadakal and Halebid in Karnataka, showing scenes from the war at Kurukshetra

bloodshed at Kurukshetra is not about property or vengeance; it is about restoring humanity, outgrowing animal instincts, and discovering the divine.

Krishna does not fight in this war. He serves only as charioteer and guide. He can only encourage; the action is left to the Pandavas. It is their battle, their action, their decision. All he does, before the war starts, is to remind them that the war is not about property or vengeance. It is about restoring dharma and dharma is about sharing; about giving, not taking. The war is not about conquering material reality; that is a delusion for material reality can never be conquered. It is about realising spiritual reality through material reality. It is about questioning the very notions of property and identifying where from come greed, envy, rage and hate. It is about realising that in every human being is a frightened beast, seeking survival and significance, and knowing very well that humans can outgrow this beast as they empathise with others. This process of outgrowing the beast is the process of discovering God. This discourse of Krishna before the war is called the *Bhagavad Gita*, song of God.

The Kaurava forces are first led by the grand patriarch Bhishma who is like a father to the Pandavas. Krishna encourages his killing because Bhishma has abandoned ashrama-dharma. Like Yayati's son, Puru, he indulges the lust of his father, Shantanu, when he decides to give up sex so that his old father can marry the woman he loves. Though never married, he lives as a householder taking care of his nephews and his grandnephews. Even when the grandnephews, the Pandavas and Kauravas, are old enough to take charge, in an overprotective zeal, he refuses to gracefully withdraw and continues to participate in worldly affairs.

When it emerges that killing Bhishma is impossible since he

Kerala mural showing Parashurama, the warrior-priest incarnation of Vishnu

has the power to choose the time of his death, Krishna encourages the Pandava Arjuna to shoot a hundred arrows and pin the old man to the ground and immobilise him. Thus Krishna forcibly removes the incorrigible Bhishma from the arena of society.

After Bhishma, the Kauravas are led by their teacher, Drona, who is also teacher to the Pandavas. Krishna encourages Drona's killing because Drona has abandoned varna-dharma. Though born in a family of priests, he functions as a warrior and even crowns his son king of a kingdom created by laying claim to one half of Draupada's land. As teacher, he teaches his students everything about war and nothing about peace. He teaches his students about taking property rather than sharing property. He teaches them everything about material reality and nothing about spiritual reality.

And so, Krishna encourages the Pandava Yudhishtira to tell a white lie and declare that Ashwatthama is dead. 'You will refer to Ashwatthama, the elephant, but he will assume it is Ashwatthama, his son. Heartbroken, he will stop fighting, and when he stops fighting,' says Krishna, 'Draupadi's brother, Dhristadhyumna, can sever his head from his body as he severed Draupada's kingdom of Panchala.'

After Drona, Karna is raised to the position of commander. Both Karna and Krishna know that Karna is the child of Kunti, born before her marriage to Pandu. He is therefore the elder brother of the Pandavas, Krishna's eldest cousin, who was raised amongst charioteers.

Karna manages to learn archery from Parashurama and becomes a renowned archer in the Kaurava court. Draupadi refused to let him contest for her hand in marriage because of his association with charioteers, and the Pandavas revile him

An angry Bhima preparing to disembowel Dusshasana and drink his blood.

Bhima and Duryodhana raise their maces and prepare to fight the final battle.

Photographs of Kathakali performances

constantly because of his low social status, but Duryodhana treats him like a prince. Draupadi's action costs her dearly. She rejects a charioteer only to end up marrying five men who gamble her away. Duryodhana's affection costs Karna dearly; he is forced to choose between a friend and dharma. Karna chooses his friend.

And so God turns against him. In the heat of battle his chariot wheel gets stuck in the ground. As he jumps down to release the wheel, Krishna encourages Arjuna to shoot the unarmed helpless Karna in his back. Arjuna protests but Krishna insists. A man who allowed the helpless Draupadi to be abused, a man who chose friendship over dharma, has no right to claim protection under dharma.

Bhishma, Drona and Karna are all students of Parashurama. Each one is taught warfare to uphold dharma. But each one remains silent when Draupadi is being disrobed in public. Each one of them justifies, however regretfully, their support of the Kauravas over Pandavas. Ultimately, they focus on rules rather than the spirit of dharma. Ultimately, they focus on their own helplessness rather than the consequences of their actions on society at large. That is why, as Krishna, Vishnu engineers the killing of his own students.

KRISHNA SILENTLY WITNESSES THE KILLING of each and every Kaurava by the Pandava Bhima. He watches as Bhima drinks the blood of Dusshasana, Duryodhana's brother who had disrobed Draupadi. He watches Bhima wash Draupadi's hair, untied during that horrific incident, with Dusshasana's blood and tie it with Dusshasana's entrails. Thus a vile vow taken

The songs of the Ashta-Chaap poets, including Surdas, is sung for Srinathji.

Narayaniyam composed by Melpathur Narayana Bhattathiri is sung at Guruvayoor.

Songs of Haridasa devotional poets are sung for Chennakeshava.

Songs of Tukaram are sung in praise of Vithal.

Krishna enshrined in (clockwise) Nathdvara, Rajasthan; Guruvayoor, Kerala; Pandharpur, Maharashtra; and Udupi, Karnataka

thirteen years ago in the gambling hall is fulfilled.

When it becomes difficult to kill Duryodhana, Krishna encourages the breaking of a war-rule: never strike the enemy below the waist. Bhima strikes Duryodhana below the waist and breaks his thighs.

With the hundredth Kaurava killed, the Pandavas are declared victorious. They are now masters not only of Indraprastha, the kingdom they built, but also of Hastinapur, the kingdom of their ancestors that they should have inherited.

But victory comes at a price. Following the eighteen-day war, Drona's son, Ashwatthama, attacks the Pandava camp at night and kills the five children of Draupadi, mistaking them to be the Pandavas. As God, Krishna knew this would happen but he does not stop it, perhaps to remind the Pandavas of the consequences of any war, even one fought for dharma.

And so, in the end, Krishna has to console two women: Gandhari, the mother of the Kauravas, and Draupadi, the wife of the Pandavas. Both have lost their children.

Gandhari curses Krishna and his family. Krishna lets her. In that fit of rage, all the bitterness in Gandhari's heart gushes out leaving behind a soul once again pure for love. Gandhari then weeps uncontrollably for her imperfect children. Krishna holds her tight, feeling her pain.

Krishna also feels Draupadi's pain. The battle which avenges her humiliation also claims all five of her children. Draupadi learns that both vengeance and justice come at a price. Krishna asks her to forgive and let go. It is difficult. He holds her in his arms and gives her strength. Life is difficult and people are imperfect. Unable to cope with the vagaries of this world, everyone makes mistakes. True love is the ability to love people

Rajagopalswamy from Tamil Nadu, Nayaka period

despite their mistakes.

IN THE FINAL CHAPTER OF the *Mahabharata*, Yudhishtira is indignant when he finds the Kauravas in heaven. 'How can they — the cause of so much suffering — be given a place in heaven?' Krishna retorts, 'You killed them in battle and ruled their lands and still you hate them? You claim to have renounced the world but you have not renounced your rage. How then can you stake a claim to heaven?'

In the Hindu world, everything is God. Everything. Even the Kauravas. Everything in the world is a part of Krishna. Everything therefore can be loved and is capable of loving. He who has truly realised Krishna cannot hate the Kauravas. He cannot hate anyone. Krishna may punish the Kauravas for their misdeeds, but he never rejects them. His love makes room for the weakest, the cruellest, the most imperfect. This is dharma.

When we stop loving, we embrace adharma. We judge, condemn and reject people. Invalidate them in hatred. We stop being generous. Like the Kauravas, we become mean-minded, petty, stingy, clingy and possessive. Or like the Pandavas, we become clueless, confused, in search of direction and wisdom. We forget the path to Madhuvan. We entrap ourselves in Kurukshetra.

The earth weeps for us. Because in our inability to love, in our pursuit for power, in our lack of wisdom, we lose a golden opportunity to enjoy life, make life enjoyable for others and find joy in giving joy. That is why the Krishna saga begins when the earth-cow stands before Vishnu and begs him to save her children.

God listens. The cowherd turns into the charioteer. He

Poster art showing Radha and Krishna

disciplines the unruly horses of the head with verses of the *Bhagavad Gita*. The verses provide a true understanding of life, an understanding that prevents false interpretations of circumstances and false expectations from the world. Thus enlightened, the heart loses its craving for power and embraces love. We participate in life, not to control it, but to appreciate it.

The charioteer Krishna of the *Mahabharata*, lord of Rukmini, appeals to our head and helps us in times of crisis. He transforms our world from a battlefield into a garden. He leads us out of Kurukshetra and helps us return to Madhuvan.

There we find the cowherd Krishna of the *Bhagavata*, lord of Radha, who appeals to our heart, and awakens a desire for celebration. Senses stirred, heart rejoicing in love, head filled with wisdom, we submit innocently to his music and take our place in his Maha-raas.

7

KALKI'S SECRET

Allow things to wane

Balarama holds a pestle called Sunanda, used for pounding grain.

Balarama holds a plough for tilling the land which is why he is called Hala-yudha, the warrior who fights with a plough.

Balarama is fair with smooth hair, and a simpleton.

Krishna is dark with curly hair and a mischievous romantic rake.

In Jain traditions, Balarama is more revered than Krishna and is addressed as the wise and non-violent Baladeva.

Two 19th-century Kalighat paintings from Bengal

When telling the story of the *Mahabharata*, parents often forget to tell their children a very important detail. That Balarama, Krishna's elder brother, refused to participate in the war. While Krishna led the Pandavas to victory on the battlefields of Kurukshetra, Balarama was away on a pilgrimage, unable to make sense of the carnage.

In some scriptures, Balarama is an avatar of Vishnu's serpent, Sesha, accompanying Vishnu when the latter descends on earth. But in other scriptures, especially those from south India, he is an incarnation of Vishnu, the ninth of the ten avatars. He is shown holding agricultural implements such as the plough and the pestle, unlike Krishna who holds implements of animal husbandry. This suggests that in early India, the two gods were gods associated with primary economic activities and that later, they acquired deeper metaphysical significance, but always complementing each other.

Through Krishna, Vishnu embraces worldliness or pravritti-marga, while through Balarama, Vishnu embraces monasticism or nivritti-marga. Though Balarama is the elder brother of Krishna, in the list of incarnations, he comes after Krishna, suggesting perhaps that in the lore of Vishnu, Balarama's approach is not as preferred as Krishna's.

Balarama is not a shrewd diplomat like his younger brother, nor is he the romantic rake. In the temple in Puri, Orissa, Krishna is worshipped as Jagannath, lord of the world, alongside his younger sister, Subhadra, and his elder brother, Balarama. While in the traditional narrative Balarama is married to Revati and has a daughter called Vatsala, in the Puri temple tradition he is treated almost like an ascetic who, like Shiva, likes bhang, a drink made using narcotic Indian hemp, and shuns the company

Traditional dolls of Jagannath and his siblings, brother Balabhadra and sister Subhadra

of women. This disengagement from women in metaphysical terms indicates a withdrawal from material reality. While Krishna struggles with the Pandavas to hold on to dharma, Balarama simply lets go. He goes away on pilgrimage and allows things to collapse. Balarama is thus more Shiva-like than Vishnu-like, and as the ninth avatar, after Krishna, he seems to herald the end of the world.

Like Shiva who supports Devas and Asuras equally, Balarama supports the Pandavas and the Kauravas equally. He trains both Bhima and Duryodhana in the art of fighting with a mace. Since he feels Krishna sides with the Pandavas, he tries to balance things by favouring Duryodhana over Bhima. On his return from his pilgrimage, he learns that Bhima killed Duryodhana by breaking a rule of mace-warfare: he had struck below the navel, and smashed Duryodhana's thigh. In fury, he raises his plough determined to strike and punish Bhima. But Krishna stops his elder brother, reminds him the war is over, and that for dharma, sometimes, rules have to be broken. Rules exist to protect the helpless; Duryodhana has misused the rules to abuse helpless Draupadi, hence has lost the moral right to claim protection under the rules. Balarama sees sense in Krishna's words and lowers his plough.

Balarama is a passionate god. He gets angry easily and is appeased as easily. He is also a simpleton. All these are also traits of Shiva. He does not understand the machinations of Krishna. He does not understand Krishna's complex logic, expressed in the *Bhagavad Gita*, justifying the war. He does not appreciate the notion of property. For him wisdom lies in renouncing property altogether.

But Balarama trusts Krishna. He knows there is wisdom in

Images showing Krishna and Shiva in their distinctive stances;

Poster art showing the death of Krishna

his younger brother's words. Perhaps there is another way to live, with property, by outgrowing the attachment for property. This can only happen not by shunning desire but by engaging with desire and exploring the roots of territorial behaviour.

IN THE *MAHABHARATA*, AT THE end of the war in Kurukshetra, Krishna is cursed by Gandhari, the mother of the Kauravas. Though Krishna has helped re-establish dharma, he has also broken a mother's heart by not sparing even one of her hundred sons. Gandhari curses Krishna that he will witness the killing of his own children and grandchildren and relatives and see his city fall.

The curse realises itself thirty-six years later. Krishna, and Balarama, watch their entire clan destroy itself in a mindless civil war ignited by an argument as to who was right and who was wrong in Kurukshetra. After this, Balarama loses all will to live; his life slips out of his mouth in the form of a serpent. Shortly after Balarama's death, Krishna dies too; he is shot dead by a hunter who mistakes his toe for the snout of a deer and shoots a poisoned arrow.

The hunter's arrow strikes Krishna on the sole of his left foot. Normally, in images, while playing the flute, Krishna always stands on his left foot and swings his right foot across. This is the opposite of Shiva's typical posture; Shiva stands on his right foot and swings his left foot across. The left foot represents material reality because it belongs to the side of the beating heart while the right foot represents spiritual reality because it belongs to the stiller, more silent, opposite side. Krishna stands firmly on the left foot, but also places the right foot on the ground, indicating grounding in material reality giving cognisance to

The robes are embellished with designs, suggesting the artist's discomfort with monastic ideals of simplicity.

Kalamkari print of Buddha

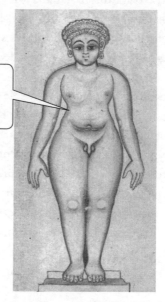

In the Puranas, Buddha is often confused with all monks, including Jain ascetics who wear no clothes.

Mysore painting of Buddha

spiritual reality. Shiva, on the other hand, balances his entire body on the right foot, indicating his clear preference for spiritual reality alone, making him Shiva-Ekapada, Shiva who stands on one foot.

At the time of his death, Krishna took an opposite stance; he swung his left foot over the right, exposing the left sole. In other words, as his time on earth as Krishna came to an end, Vishnu abandoned pravritti-marga represented by the left foot and embraced nivritti-marga represented by the right foot. The world-embracing that characterised his earlier avatars now had to wane because the Dvapara yuga had come to an end and the Kali yuga, the fourth and final quarter of the world, had dawned.

IN THE MORE POPULAR LIST of the ten avatars of Vishnu, the ninth avatar is shown as Buddha, not Balarama. Some Hindu scriptures say Vishnu descended as Buddha out of compassion for animals to stop the practice of animal sacrifices and to promote non-violence and vegetarianism. Others say Vishnu took the form of the Buddha to distract people from Vedic practices, to prepare the world for its imminent destruction.

Buddhists do not accept either of these claims; they see it as an attempt by shrewd Hindu storytellers to make Buddhism a subsect of Hinduism. From a historical point of view, the inclusion of Buddha as an avatar of Vishnu does seem to have political motivation, but from a philosophical point of view, the Buddha-avatar indicates a step closer to the end of the world.

In the Rig Veda it is said that desire is the root of creation. Because spiritual reality (Narayana) desired to know himself, Brahma bloomed out of Vishnu's lotus and Brahmanda,

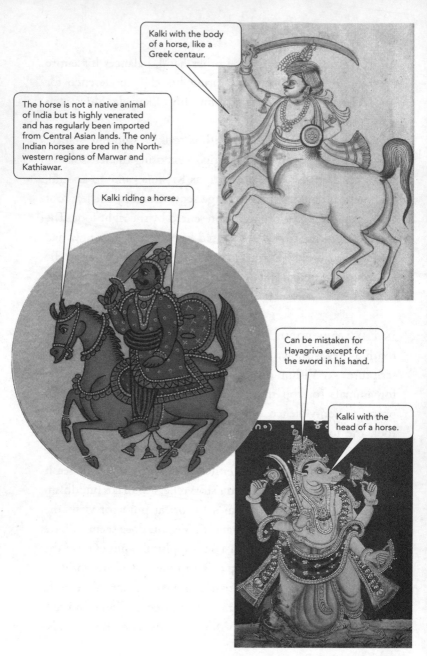

Three visual representations of Kalki in Mysore art

Brahma's world, came into being. Thus Kama, or desire, is a living, giving force. But in Buddhist mythology, Kama is Mara, the demon of desire. He is the root cause of all suffering. If one wants liberation from all suffering, one must abandon all desire. When this happens, all engagement stops, life ceases to be. This is the monastic path, the nivritti-marga which ultimately leads to what the Buddhists call nirvana, blowing out of the flame, an idea similar to the Hindu notion of moksha, liberation from the cycle of rebirths.

When there is no desire, Narayana would not wake up and Shiva would not open his eyes to the splendour of Prakriti. The Goddess would remain unacknowledged. There would be no Maya, no Brahmanda, no subjective reality, no human observation of nature, no flowering of human consciousness, just Prakriti without Purusha. This disengagement of the two metaphysical realities is described as destruction.

While Buddha and/or Balarama represents destruction by passive withdrawal from the world, Kalki represents active destruction of the world. He is the tenth and final avatar of Vishnu, visualised as a warrior who rides a white horse and brandishes a flaming sword.

The story of Kalki starts appearing in Hindu scriptures at the time when India was overrun by a whole host of foreign marauders from Central Asia. These were brutal and barbaric tribes such as the Huns and later the Mongols. The story was a clear response to their brutality. These new invaders were destroying the old way of life and it was hoped that Vishnu, as Kalki, would destroy the new ways, and restore life to the old

Bronze images of the traditional five human avatars of Vishnu

ways. Kalki was probably inspired by messianic thoughts that is prevalent in Judaism, Christianity and Islam. He was the deliverer and the saviour.

Across India, there are many folk heroes who ride a horse and brandish a sword much like Kalki. He is thus almost a guardian god in folk imagination, but in the scriptures, he is the one who will close the Kalpa, the world-cycle, so that a new one can begin.

Even the Buddhists had a similar idea, of a Bodhisattva of the future, Manjushri, who yields a flaming sword. In the Tibetan Buddhist tradition, this wrathful manifestation Manjushri is called Yamantaka. Yamantaka is an epithet associated with Shiva in Hindu tradition and means the destroyer of death. Thus, metaphysically, Kalki will destroy everything, even death. He will destroy all structures so that none exist. In other words, he will herald Pralaya.

Material reality is impermanent. It has to change; in other words, it has to die and be reborn. So everything that has form and name has to eventually wither away and die. In the lore of Vishnu these transformations of Prakriti are not random; they are organised and predictable. They take the form of yugas, or eras. Just as every living organism goes through four phases of life — childhood, youth, maturity and old age — so does the world. Krita yuga marks the childhood of the world, Kali yuga marks the youth, Dvapara marks the maturity of the world and Treta, its old age. Parashurama heralds the end of Krita, Ram the end of Treta, Krishna the end of Dvapara, and Kalki the end of Kali yuga. Pralaya is death, death before rebirth. Pralaya is when Vishnu goes to sleep, becomes Narayana. Pralaya is when Ananta becomes Sesha, infinity becomes zero and Yoga-maya becomes Yoga-nidra.

Calendar art showing milkmaids weeping as Krishna leaves Vrindavan

Photograph showing the Ratha-yatra festival of Puri, Orissa

Vishnu thus acknowledges the end of the world, engages with it, even participates in it. While as Parashurama and Ram and Krishna, he struggles to hold on to dharma, despite the corrupting march of time, as Balarama and finally Kalki, he lets go and allows the world to collapse. This is wisdom, knowing when to act and when to withdraw, knowing when to stop fighting and allowing age to take its toll.

THE IDEA OF THINGS ENDING recurs in the three great epics of India: *Ramayana*, *Mahabharata* and *Bhagavata*. In the *Ramayana*, in the end, Sita returns to the earth whence she came from and Ram walks into the river Sarayu, never to rise up again. In the *Mahabharata*, in the end, the Pandavas have to renounce their kingdom and walk up the mountains, seeking heaven and ultimately facing death. In the *Bhagavata*, Krishna leaves the village of cowherds, Vrindavan, and makes his way to the city of Mathura. He leaves on a chariot whose charioteer's name is Akrura, one who is not cruel. The milkmaids beg Krishna to stay back but Krishna moves on to the next phase of his life, abandoning his parents and friends and lovers. That the charioteer is 'not-cruel' is a clear communication that one must never begrudge the march of time. Like Yashoda, who raised Krishna with love and affection only to watch him leave her and go to Mathura, we must all ultimately learn to let go.

In a way, Akrura is Yama, the god of death, described in mythology as dispassionate. Yama evokes fear in all of us. But Yama himself does not seek to frighten; he has no feelings. He is merely doing his duty as the one who separates material reality from spiritual reality. The journey which begins in the mother's

Kama, god of love, shoots an arrow that will inflame the five senses.

Miniature painting of Kama

Yama, god of death, rides a buffalo that moves steadily towards all living creatures and will eventually catch up with them.

Cambodian stone carving of Yama

The wheel and the mace associated with inevitability and pain are symbols of Yama in Vishnu's arms.

The conch and lotus flower associated with water and life are symbols of Kama in Vishnu's arms.

Benarasi wooded doll of Vishnu

womb ends with the arrival of Yama. In the mother's womb, thanks to Kama, the god of love, spiritual reality interacts with and is wrapped in material reality. But a time comes when Yama must unwrap the material reality and release spiritual reality.

Both Kama and Yama are forms of Vishnu, doing their duty, preserving the cycle of rebirths. Kama ignites life. Yama ignites death. Kama ensures death is not permanent; Yama ensures life is not permanent. There are typically no temples dedicated to Kama or Yama but their images are sometimes seen in Vishnu temples. Kama is depicted riding a parrot and holding a sugarcane bow in his hand; Yama rides a buffalo and holds in his hand either a book of accounts or a staff or a noose. Kama arouses the senses, makes Brahma succumb to the power of Maya; Yama ensures that all actions are repaid, thus maintaining the account book of Karma.

The symbols of Kama and Yama are found on the image of Vishnu. Vishnu holds in his hands four symbols: Shankha (conch), Chakra (wheel), Gada (mace) and Padma (lotus). Shanka symbolises communication; Chakra marks the wheel of time; Gada the demand for discipline; Padma the nectar of joy. Shankha and Padma are water symbols; they affirm life and love and so are associated with Kama. Chakra and Gada are fire symbols; they affirm the rhythm of nature and the rules of culture and so are associated with Yama. Together, Kama and Yama preserve life. Together, Kama and Yama make up Vishnu.

A LITTLE KNOWN CHARACTER IN Hindu mythology is Vadavagni, a mare which breathes fire and stands on the ocean floor. This submarine mare causes the sea water to evaporate and

South Indian painting of Kalki

turn into mist, thus preventing the sea from ever overflowing on to land. It is said that at the time of Pralaya, Vadavagni will stop doing this, causing the ocean to expand and submerge the earth. The fire of the submarine mare will burst forth in the form of volcanoes. Everything will be destroyed by lava and water.

The origin of the fire-breathing mare is interesting. According to one story, Kama, the god of love, once tried to arouse desire in the mind of Shiva. Shiva opened his third eye, released a missile of fire and destroyed the god of desire. But without desire, the world cannot function. Hence, Vishnu caught the fire of Shiva's third-eye, turned it into a mare and hid her under the sea.

The horse is a highly revered animal in Hinduism right from Rig Vedic times even though, strangely, the horse is not a native Indian animal. It does not thrive in the subcontinent except in parts of Gujarat and Rajasthan. Since the horse came into India from the North West frontier, along with traders and marauders, Vishnu's horse-riding form, Kalki, has been associated with warlords who overran India in medieval times.

Vishnu not only rides a horse. He also becomes a horse. One form of Vishnu with the head of a horse that is highly revered especially in south India is Hayagriva. This form of Vishnu is associated with education. From the horse's head emerges Saraswati, goddess of knowledge.

Vedic mythology is full of tales where wisdom reaches the world through horse-headed beings. The sun, for example, appeared with a horse's head to reveal the wisdom of the Veda to Rishi Yagnavalkya. Rishi Dadichi replaced his human head with a horse's so that he could share Vedic wisdom with the Ashwini twins.

What is this Vedic wisdom? Vedic wisdom is the realisation

Patta painting from Orissa showing the horse-headed Hayagriva and his consort, identified as Lakshmi

that there is more to life than material reality that is perceived through the senses. It is wisdom that liberates us from the limitations of nature. It enables man to break free from Prakriti and realise Purusha. Prakriti makes us mortal and restless, Purusha makes us immortal and serene. The journey from Brahma to brahman, from the finite to the infinite, is the song of Hayagriva.

When Brahma was born, the first emotion he experienced was curiosity — who was he and why was he? Curiosity was followed by fear, because he found no answers. This fear is different from the fear of animals. Animals are afraid of scarcity, animals are afraid of predators, but these are real fears. Human fear is born of imagination — imagined scarcity, imagined predators and more importantly an imagined idea of self-worth. This self-worth is determined by possessions, 'what I have' rather than 'what I am'. Self worth rises as one possesses more wealth, more power over others and more information.

Hayagriva draws attention to the fact that the notion of property is not an objective reality, but a subjective truth, a cultural construction of human beings, not a natural phenomenon. In other words, they are creations of Maya and components of Brahmanda. If man does not exist, there would be no property to possess. Nature does not need man; man needs nature. It is a delusion of man that it is the master of nature, and the owner of nature's wealth and information.

When we self-aggrandise ourselves by being territorial and dominating other human beings, Hayagriva reminds us that we are still animals, displaying animal instincts of survival, and that we have not evolved despite a larger human brain. Vedic wisdom is that which enables man to break free from the animal and

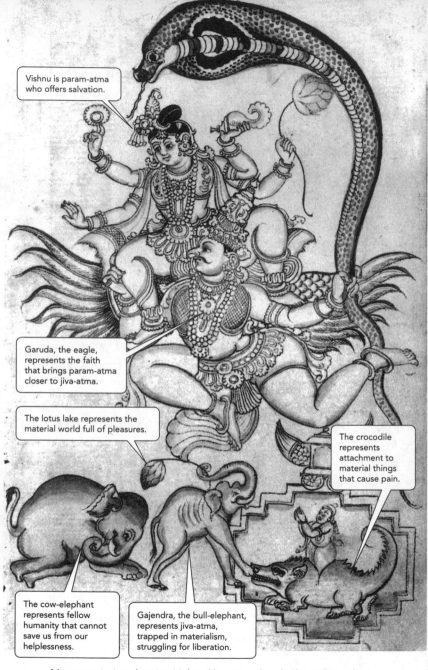

Mysore painting showing Vishnu liberating the elephant Gajendra

discover the human. To break free from fear and discover faith. For that, we have to surrender to the idea of spiritual reality, to Purusha, that which exists beyond Prakriti.

Vishnu lore tells us the story of the elephant-king, Gajendra, who was sporting in a lotus pond with a herd of cow-elephants who adored him. Suddenly, a crocodile caught hold of his foot and began dragging him underwater. Gajendra thrashed about in the water and tried to get rid of the crocodile but the crocodile did not release his grip. The cow-elephants tried to rescue him but failed. He was helpless until he picked up a lotus and begged Vishnu to come to his aid.

The story draws attention to the human condition. We are all Gajendras. Sometimes, like Devas, we crave for material security. Even when we get it we become insecure. Insecurity breeds hedonism or may transform into complacency and cynicism as one finds oneself bereft of any purpose. At other times, like Asuras, we crave for material growth. It becomes the sole purpose of existence. When we grow materially we become arrogant and feel invulnerable, until circumstances turn against us. In misery, we thrash about like Gajendra trying to get rid of the crocodile. No one comes to our rescue. No one can come to our rescue. We become restless and anxious. Liberation from this state will come only when we surrender to the wisdom of Vishnu, revealed through his stories, symbols and rituals.

ACKNOWLEDGEMENTS

I would like to thank all those who helped in the making of the book including:

- R.N. Singh and Dharmendra Rao of Ramsons Kalapratishtana, Mysore, for their unwavering support. Most of the handicraft images in this book were provided by them.

- Harsha Dehejia for helping me with the image of Balarama and Yamuna.

- Swapnil Sakpal, for helping with the artwork.